Praise for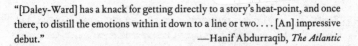

"[Daley-Ward] has a knack for getting directly to a story's heat-point, and once there, to distill the emotions within it down to a line or two.... [An] impressive debut."   —Hanif Abdurraqib, *The Atlantic*

"Yrsa's work is like holding the truth in your hands. It sweats and breathes before you.... A glorious living thing."

—Florence Welch, of Florence + the Machine

"*bone* opens with a small explosion.... The poems that follow pick up the dual meaning ... of threat and of erotic desire. Often, the two are intertwined.... Excellent."   —*The Paris Review* (staff pick)

"Who decided that only a picture can paint a thousand words? ... [Daley-Ward] examines the alchemy between mind and body—with subjects ranging from trauma to hunger to desire."   —*Elle*

"Daley-Ward's short poems cover subjects like depression, falling in and out of love, and sexuality with a fierce staccato that, as the title suggests, cuts deep."

—*Vogue*

"[*bone* is] the one poetry book every young Black girl will appreciate.... [With] poems that touch the heart, question societal norms, and talk about the complexity of sexuality, [Yrsa Daley-Ward has written] a book of great depth."

—*Essence*

"Another stunning excavator of human heat and light, Yrsa Daley-Ward goes straight to the messy beating heart of animal attraction with *bone*, mesmerizing poems that strip bare the pain and beauty of negotiating longing, sex, and love."

—*HuffPost*

"The perfect title for a book that looks for that hard place between the will and the flesh.... *bone* is a bounty of passionate and pained lines, narrators whose hearts have been turned, twisted, and sometimes stomped, but who remain open and willing—because how else could we live?"

—*The Millions*, "Must-Read Poetry"

"[*bone*] is an interrogation of self, offering a lyrical autopsy on the manner in which we are harmed by the traumas of those who share our dark skin, female gender, and cultural displacement." —*Vice*

"Daley-Ward has become a powerful voice of Black womanhood, speaking of her experiences and wisdom gleaned from growing up as a first-generation British woman of African and Caribbean heritage." —*Dazed*

"[Yrsa Daley-Ward] is at the realm of a new wave of contemporary poets who inspire an unprecedented level of empathy and accessibility through their honest and raw approach. . . . [A] powerful collection of a woman facing tumultuous inner and external battles head-on, delivered with a hard-hitting directness, yet with inflections of optimism throughout that are bound to touch readers to their core." —*i-D*

"The actor, author, model, and poet draws from her own experiences as well as issues affecting today's society throughout her work and is truly a storyteller ('some tall, some dark') of the soul." —*POPSUGAR*

"Inspiringly relatable, Daley-Ward's poetry voices acknowledgment and validity. The transparency of exposed darkness is clothed in pretty, but still effective, verses that pack empowering womanly sass." —Saint Heron, "14 Books to Add to Your Library"

Praise for *The Terrible*

LONGLISTED FOR THE 2019 PEN OPEN BOOK AWARD

"Devastating and lyrical." —*The New York Times*

"Though her plainspokenness resembles Rupi Kaur's accessibility, Daley-Ward has a specific story to tell, one that is suspenseful and affecting in its details." —*The New Yorker*

"A coming-of-age memoir . . . of particular lyricism and bracing honesty."
—*The New York Times Book Review*

"A powerful, unconventionally structured memoir recounting harrowing coming-of-age ordeals . . . Daley-Ward resists classification in this profound mix of poetry and prose. . . . [She] has quite a ferociously moving story to tell."
—*Kirkus* (starred review)

"I tore through Yrsa Daley-Ward's poetic memoir *The Terrible* in a matter of hours. . . . An impressive take on the memoir that prioritizes emotion over event."
—*The Paris Review* (staff pick)

"Profoundly beautiful . . . [Daley-Ward] interweaves verse and prose to great effect, offering less a simple retelling of her life, and more of an impression of it, a sense of how it must feel to live it. Much of what Daley-Ward recounts of her childhood is devastating . . . and she has a unique ability to tell these parts of her life with an unflinching intensity, the kind that sears itself onto your skin; and yet this is not a story without hope or love."
—*NYLON*

"Absolutely stunning . . . a poetic look at someone's life."
—Lauren Christensen, *CBS This Morning*

"[Yrsa Daley-Ward] makes the emotional brutality of dealing with family, adolescence, addiction, and sexuality accessible to her readers. . . . She continually incorporates gut-wrenching imagery in her work, and in both *bone* and *The Terrible*, she packages heightened emotion into just one or two lines."
—*Ploughshares*

"Unflinching . . . *The Terrible*'s raw yet lilting prose draws the reader in at once. Unpredictable shifts in form and structure—from prose to poetry and script—are refreshingly disorientating. This is both a defiant book and a defiantly inventive one."
—*The Times Literary Supplement* (London)

"Open up the first page of Yrsa Daley-Ward's genre-defying memoir, and you'll find yourself immediately transfixed by her rhythmic language. Daley-Ward unspools the story of her difficult coming-of-age as it *felt*, forgoing the pacing of a conventional memoir for something more poetic and visceral. . . . In this book, her unique voice has room to grow roots on the page."
—Refinery29

PENGUIN BOOKS

THE HOW

Yrsa Daley-Ward is a writer and poet of mixed Jamaican and Nigerian heritage and is the author of *bone* and *The Terrible*, the winner of the PEN Ackerley Prize. She splits her time between Brooklyn and London.

THE HOW

Notes on the Great Work

of Meeting Yourself

YRSA DALEY-WARD

PENGUIN BOOKS

PENGUIN BOOKS
An imprint of Penguin Random House LLC
penguinrandomhouse.com

LIBRARY OF CONGRESS CATALOGING-IN-PUBLICATION DATA
Names: Daley-Ward, Yrsa, author.
Title: The how: notes on the great work of meeting yourself / Yrsa Daley-Ward.
Description: New York: Penguin Books [2021]
Identifiers: LCCN 2021010716 (print) | LCCN 2021010717 (ebook) |
ISBN 9780143135609 (paperback) | ISBN 9780525507253 (ebook)
Subjects: LCSH: Self-actualization (Psychology) | Mind and body.
Classification: LCC BF637.S4 D345 2021 (print) |
LCC BF637.S4 (ebook) | DDC 158.1—dc23
LC record available at https://lccn.loc.gov/2021010716
LC ebook record available at https://lccn.loc.gov/2021010717

Printed in the United States of America
2nd Printing

BOOK DESIGN BY LUCIA BERNARD

for us.

The Content

A) THE HOW (mythical)

Noun. An antidote to existential dread, disconnection, or despair. A miraculous event or happening that will make you feel less empty forever and ever and ever. Amen.

B) THE HOW (practical)

Noun. A pursuit, action, or doing that will change your life, ~~even~~ especially during these uncertain times.

C) THE HOW (material)

Noun. A thing that, once acquired, will absolutely make you Better.

D) THE HOW (spiritual)

Noun. A belief or practice (religious or otherwise) that will add meaning, color, and vigor to an otherwise bland and confusing existence.

E) THE HOW (sustainable)

None of the above. A loose and shifting guide toward even more of all the things you are.

Introduction

(i)

We are afraid of small things. Large things. Dead things. Things that are living and persistent. Things that we must do but keep putting off. Legal and numerical things. Filthy, delicious things, so deadly they seem like fun. Things that move gently and in secret. Slow-moving things. Ill health. Death. Things like The End of the World. Things that we don't and will never control. Things that will almost certainly happen, and things that may not.

I see you and I recognize your fear. You see me and you understand mine. We are accustomed to its moving shapes and many sounds and we have been living among each other for too long to not understand that we have them in common. Though our specifics vary, our fears are family. When we open our mouths to speak, fear scratches at our throats, and then it is carelessly present, turning the air a grim and unremarkable color. This is why there are times that we avoid each other. You remind me of myself—of my uncertainty and anxiety and all the other painful things that I'm afraid to look at. When I catch your eye, I am often alarmed at my own tender reflection.

Fear itself is hardly the enemy. Fear is, in fact, an excellent indicator of where we are and what we believe to be true. It is too much to watch it at work sometimes. It's uncomfortable to see the fear escaping our lips, reverberating in the space between us. It is obscuring our view, and everything about our lives. And I am tired—and are you tired?

Every single day of our lives, we are sold "remedies." We are sold all these urgent methods to disguise the fear. So many that we get confused. So many that our heads are spinning, and we can't tell our own thoughts from those that are coming from outside. You can't see what you want to do. I can't tell what I want to be, or care about. Wherever we go, TV and books and advertisements shout out what to do to conquer this fear, what to do to feel more alive. HOW to be *good*. How to be better. How to survive. How to stay in charge and inside of your body. How to feed and preserve your body. How to dress your body and sell it. How to succeed, leaving others behind in the dust.

These hows and how-tos are everywhere we look, in every place of retail, fitness, worship, and entertainment. These hows are flexible and glossy, know how to live, and keep getting all of our money. They tell us exactly what to buy, and where to buy it. They sound like promises and they look like lifelines. We are obsessed with them, because they are flawless and stylish, fitter and cleaner than us, highly curated, and frighteningly relevant. They are political. They do superior activism, think critically, have wonderful social lives, and they know how to organize. We see pictures of them on their backs in impossible, sun-filled locations. They succeed and prosper, while the rest of us are simply getting by. Just.

They look just like us; that's the problem. These hows are extremely vulnerable when it pays to be, and tremendously private. Perhaps they bought the house you have always wanted, perhaps they have the partner of your dreams. They are saintly and sexy with hidden limits. They are oh so perfect, and of course, they are a lie.

These hows will evade you, and they are built to do so; to keep you on the outside looking in, impressionable and wanting. They are so loud and fast and distracting that it is impossible to keep up. Every so often you think you find a way into them, but in a matter of time, you are lost.

In a world so filled with voice, how to ever be sure of your own?

We are drowning in so many hows that we cannot find ourselves;
and when all we are told is that we do *not* know how,
all that we feel is weight.

LOSE WEIGHT NOW GAIN MORE OF YOURSELF BUT IN ALL THE RIGHT PLACES BE IN THE MOMENT PLAN FOR YOUR FUTURE GET MONEY AND THINGS STAY FIT KEEP YOUR BODY TIGHT BE LOOSE HAVE SEX FIND A RELATIONSHIP DISTRACT YOURSELF KICK THE HABIT LOOK YOUNG AND SMOOTH GROW OLD GRACEFULLY LOOK HOT ALL THE TIME LOOK AS THOUGH LOOKING HOT JUST HAPPENS TO YOU NATURALLY AND WITH NO APPARENT EFFORT BE UNIMPRESSED BUT POSITIVE DON'T CARE TOO MUCH BUT CARE ENOUGH TO BE A WORTHY HUMAN BEING BE RADICAL NOT PREACHY HAVE STRONG POLITICAL OPINIONS BUT REMAIN MALLEABLE ENOUGH TO PUT THEM ASIDE FOR THE NEXT MORE PERTINENT CAUSE BE OUTRAGED (BUT DON'T BITE THE HAND THAT FEEDS) BE CONFIDENT AND HUMBLE OUTSPOKEN BUT ON-BRAND RADICAL AND WARY NO-NONSENSE BUT SPECULATIVE REMAIN OPEN TO THE PEOPLE WHO KNOW MORE ABOUT IT THAN YOU OF WHICH THERE ARE MANY CANCEL THOSE WHO ARE TOO SLOW ON THEIR JOURNEY TO KEEP UP WITH THE WORLD'S NEW AND EVOLVING KNOWLEDGE WORK HARD AND OF COURSE TAKE IT EASY

(ii)

We have absorbed so much of the outside. It is a mass to un-learn, a voyage back to center. When you go to list your dreams, do you draw a blank?

By and large, over time, we have talked ourselves out of what we really want. Why do we do this? Why do we talk ourselves out of our great ideas?

It begins early. As we grow, we are told that the things we want are impossible. We start to believe that what we dream of does not exist. "Who do you think you are?" our circumstances scream, as they whip us into shape.

We can hardly blame those who raise us. They do their best with what they have been taught by the people who raised them, imposing their rules, standards, and ways of living. We inherit these ideas, to a fault. We learn to be realistic and sensible, and we travel far from our imaginations. We grow, afraid to ask for those vivid, forgotten things: the things that we honestly desire. Instead, we focus on what we think we can get. The things that we end up settling for. We learn to be actors. We get used to hiding our true selves, and often, we erase our own memories, letting go of the deep wishes of the soul, abandoning what we already know. We leave ourselves behind—and, God, are we feeling it today.

Perhaps we do this because we need to survive. Perhaps we do this to ensure our safety and community, by fitting in with those around us, and their own expectations and limitations. In many environments, the safest thing to do with our bodies is to slip by unnoticed, to bloom under the radar, in secret. But secrecy has its limits.

Where can we get to, weighed down like this? How far can we travel, heavy?

We need air and light. We need a reflection of some sort; to be able to see ourselves. We need space to stretch our limbs and we need to be allowed to grow. Meaning we need to *allow ourselves* to grow. Meaning we will change along the way. To do so, we must first leave some things at the gate.

Perhaps we have to start by remembering the thing that it is human nature to forget. Before we are to hope for any one answer, we must know there is no answer beyond ourselves. Before we are to hope for the truth, we must know there are no truths but the ones that we arrive at on our own. Developing, powerful, ever-changing truths. No one has the code for anyone else. Their work is not your work. All of us are trying to get through the days with as little or as much as we think we have. Some of us feel close to giving up; some of us think we have plans. No plan is airtight, or even close. The universe will always send conditions as reminders. Light weather, strong weather, and strange things that flood the scene.

Nobody really knows much more about it than you. Not doctors, not teachers, not writers. Not people paid to coach and speak. We come for treatment, never the cure. There is no one cure; and we know it.

We come to be reassured, to be seen and understood. We come to be soothed. To know that there are others in this mess too. We come to be sure that we are more alike than not.

(iii)

Suppose you were to begin the great work of meeting yourself. Not the you that you have built up in response to your surroundings. Not the harder or softer version of yourself that you have shaped and mastered to suit your environment. Not a more acceptable you that you feel those around you might prefer. Suppose you were to uncover, piece by piece, what it is that makes you feel the most alive. The deeper, more hidden side of your nature and motivations. The velvet lining. Suppose this is The How.

Suppose our true desires and aspirations could be rediscovered and redefined, thrust upward to illuminate the ceiling. Suppose we were to discover that there is no ceiling to be found, but endlessness, amidst the new, flickering light.

Suppose we were to begin to seek out and listen to the true things written in the body. Suppose the interest became radical, and we decided to do away with the untruths. Suppose this powerful new beginning leads us toward The How.

It will not be a direct path; we can be sure of that. We want to lie to ourselves and everyone else at every turn. We don't want others to see our pain, but we give ourselves away in our behavior and most of the things we say. We are not as slick as we believe. We want to be understood and identified with, so we do not feel so isolated, but we still want to hide aspects of our lives and our greatest fears. We want to be left alone and also . . . we really don't.

Surely, we must end the lies in order to start the truth. It will take work, but you know all about work. We have all gone to work in our millions of ways and mostly, we have not even recognized it as such. We are, each of us, so fortunate, having each experienced a range of worthwhile, alarming, *work*. Whether we like it or not, the practices that we were carrying out were all the work of becoming, and they all come together in the end.

Not that we ever reach the end.

Aren't we ready for something else? Well, absolutely. We have been ready since we arrived. That's what all the discomfort is about. We feel cramped and discontented because we sense our higher purposes glimmering in the distance. We've dreamed about the possibility and depth of new, unfamiliar states. We are blessed with an outline in a dream or a wish . . . and then we wake up and kill our possibilities in the morning.

We still dream, though, don't we? We are gifted with a sure pathway into ourselves, night after night after night.

To be useful, The How must be about finding our way inside, to what truly resonates. It cannot be more invested in anything that happens on the outside. To be maintainable rather than temporary, The How must be about seeing and feeling more of what we are. To be realistic, The How must be about removing the filters.

Over these pages, you'll find notes, lists, and nudges toward your own How. Use them in whichever way you like. Allow the starting points on the following pages to give way to something more telling and personal. Let the words travel with you into something you have already half planned, or an entirely new pursuit altogether. Let the words gently remind you that, yes, you can absolutely do it. Let them coax you into whatever action is needed for things to develop. Use them on your feet or on your back, solo or with friends, and work them any way you want.

I do not claim to know anything remotely new, but I too would love to remember more of my wishes. Little by little, they float to me in the limitless black of the night.

When I wake, I see tiny clues everywhere.

THE HOW

Where You Are, What You Want

and the distance between

But *why the difficulty*, you wonder.

You're pushing twenty, thirty, forty. Life is not what you imagined.
Things are tougher than you thought. You put out the trash. You wash the dishes in the sink, but there is always more waste. Waste. More to wash, either of the house or yourself. And when will the work end? you ask yourself. When?

Everything needs upkeep, and it's tiring.
Everything needs upkeep, and it's *terrifying*.

You work and go to bed and wake up and work and go to bed and wake up . . . and then it all begins again. It all begins.

Again. You stretch. You try to work out and you try not to eat late.

You kiss better people than before and you're careful (as careful as the lonely can be . . .) of who stays, who gets in your bed. All reasonable problems. Nothing too dire.

So why do you feel so dead?

We are held in an uncomfortable space—the chasm between what we really want and what we have come to understand as *reality*. The more that we want something and are aware that we do not have it, the more despondent we feel. This trouble is yours and it is definitely also mine. Know that your inner being (the deepest part of you) recognizes the space and distance between, feels you slipping further into the crack. But it is good to feel this conflict, this vibrant sign of budding and wanting. The growing unease is how to know that you are not living your deepest wishes. That you are not in alignment with your inner truth.

When I feel the most lost and out of sorts, I know that I am in disconnection with the very voice that has carried me thus far.

I can't hear myself, nor can I think what to do next. I flip-flop. I second-guess myself. I feel unsure. My lack of confidence causes others to lose trust in me.

But how to catch the honest voice? How to lay our eyes on the truth when we are distracted, and don't know what we're looking for? First, know that the versions of yourself that are in connection with your source are present, and living and growing inside you. (It doesn't only happen in sci-fi, this multiplying of yourself. It is happening all the time:
when you trip up on yourself in some old doorway to a behavior you have outgrown,
when the pit of your stomach makes room for a powerful new instinct,
when you love, but you leave for your own good.)

What a natural gift it is to be as multidimensional as you are, to foster a steady and growing awareness of the possibilities running alongside you. What an entirely full experience it is, to exist inside the vast and fluid spectrum of our lives and capabilities. There is so much available, but a certain amount of peace must be fostered, a certain tranquility, a certain sureness and alignment with your inner being, before you feel the full range of possibility. Before you can make out the sounds.

How do we improve this listening/awareness?

If we want to thrive, the act of accessing joy right here, right now, is one of the first muscles to strengthen. There have to be things that we are happy about today, even if they are small. I maintain that this is a skill, because there is work required to conjure these up, especially if focusing on them is not intuitive to us yet. Don't worry if you're more used to spiraling or obsessing over what needs to change than thinking about the beauty. So am I. This very act is all about making new roads into yourself. Thoughts are magnetic. Begin practicing your awareness of the small things. They will make more of themselves, and they will save your life.

When gratitude lists and affirmations (the act of introducing new stories) are suggested to us, plenty of natural and understandable resistance may arise. The first time someone spoke to me about making daily gratitude lists, I rolled my eyes. It sounded so much like a cliché. Even depression felt more worthy and real to me than *gratitude*. The idea of listing the things that were going well and ignoring everything that was going wrong seemed disingenuous. As someone who considered themselves an active problem solver, I naturally tended to place my attention and focus on the difficult. I prided myself on what I'd always thought to be one of my best attributes: the dogged will and keen ability to focus on what I needed to do or change, as opposed to noticing what was already thriving and solid. More often than not, the results came at great cost. I was chasing my tail, expending energy that would have best been placed somewhere else: loving the things that were around me. Living in this moment. Affirming and creating more of that which I wanted.

And I was stubborn. How will making a list or chanting sentences in the mirror every day change my life? I wanted to know. Did I want to become all detached from reality, one of those "spiritual types" with their head in the clouds, one who simply ignores their troubles? Wasn't this an overly simplistic fix to real-life problems? It took a while, but I eventually learned that gratitude and affirmations are so effective because they are about tuning in to a new frequency. They are about perspective and the skillful management of attention. They are about creation. Further to that, they are life decisions.

Our old habits are ingrained, worn in, soft, as are the thoughts that created them. We deserve as much grace as possible in reworking them. Rest in the promise that new pathways will appear to you in the midst of these new practices, often when you least expect it. At times, it is a great feat to stay open and willing against the growing scenes of stress and difficulty, but it is all you really need in order to begin. We begin slowly, as the largest, most powerful things do.

Try it. Every day, practice writing down all the things you feel good about. A quick, regular inventory of everything that you treasure, everything that pleases you, everything that is working out for you. See if you can commit to a month of this daily practice. If you need more inspiration and accountability, do this with a partner or a group. Practice having these discussions on an email thread, or in person. Spark each other. Remind each other on those days when it feels far away. There will surely be those days,

and on those days, this is how we swim.

But Listen,
Your Life Is Telling You
What It Needs

"Your joy will come," says the universe. "So will your love, of course. But first I must show you yourself—your actions and thoughts, again and again, in the mirrors of your own life. You must come deeply to terms with yourself and know and understand your many wild and hidden parts, not simply for what they are, but what they will show you. Then you will hold them to the light, gently letting go of what must leave. You will come to know more and understand that you know even less. This is only the very beginning."

Why Is *Everything* Work?

the never-ending work of living

Once we come of age, everything suddenly feels like work. All at once, there seem to be a million steps to getting anything done. Searching for joy feels like work. Creating feels like work. Life itself feels like work. Since everything seeps into everything else, the art of arranging our lives in order to be most constructive can appear as a never-ending medley of tasks. The word *work* has been vastly confounded with struggle, with slog, with difficulty, with toil, drudgery, and grind. A lot of our ideas about work align with some toxic idea about productivity—the idea that we are simply what we produce, when what we produce is just a part of it. No wonder we don't want to *work*.

We were not designed to shuffle from point to point, merely fulfilling errands and collecting digits in the bank account. If we want to do more than survive, if we want to do more than just get through the days, an interior adjustment must take place. It is more than cognitive; it is something entirely spiritual. In some cases, we need to redefine what we think *life* is all about. In many cases, we need to redefine what we think *work* is, and to release the idea that we must suffer and struggle for the things that we want.

A degree of everyday effort is natural. We are constantly up against things that make us stretch, wonder, and sweat. Problem-solving, starting something new, keeping things up, staying away from things, pushing ourselves into new, unfamiliar territory. But we have to remember that the experience of life itself is as important as the doings. Movement and stillness. Eating and breathing. Talking, tending, and loving.

There is much to learn about our inner selves; much *work*, and not all of it will feel amazing. But it does not have to mean strain. We can breathe deeply the whole way through, even when it is nipping at our harder memories and tender points. We can proceed with gentleness and intent. In doing so, we will shake ourselves loose.

In doing so, we are allowing more varied and encompassing types of love and expression, more honesty, deeper inspiration, and we are able to take larger risks with our hearts, careers, and minds.

On a piece of paper, note the "work" you are looking forward to doing. Now note every single type of work that scares you.

Note the work you would say that you are currently doing. Now note the work you think you *must* do, whether you are excited about it or not. Are there overlaps? Patterns? Surprises?

Who wants to do all of this? Who has time for it? *We do.* Wherever we are, let's start from there.

LOOKING AT WAYS IN WHICH WE SHORTCHANGE
OURSELVES. SETTING ASIDE WHAT FAMILY AND FRIENDS
EXPECT OF US. PRIORITIZING OUR HEALTH. NOTICING
WHAT BEAUTY SURROUNDS US. GETTING THINGS OUT
AND DOWN ON PAPER. BEGINNING THE LONG ROAD OF
BECOMING ABSOLUTELY ACCOUNTABLE. PLEASURE
SEEKING AND GIVING. MORE CONNECTION WITH THE
BODY. ASKING FOR HELP. DEEP, INTENTIONAL REST.
MOVING ON FROM OLD THINGS. DECIDING THE
CONDITIONS IN WHICH WE WISH TO LIVE. HAVING THE
COURAGE TO BECOME MORE SPECIFIC ABOUT THOSE
CONDITIONS, BECOMING EVEN MORE AUTONOMOUS IN
EVERY CORNER OF OUR EXPERIENCE. MAKING AND
SPENDING MORE TIME WITH LOVED ONES. INTUITIVE
AND GENUINE FORMS OF ACTIVISM. LEARNING HEALTHY
BOUNDARIES, EVEN IN SERVICE TO EACH OTHER.
HOLDING THOSE BOUNDARIES, EVEN WHEN IT IS
UNCOMFORTABLE. ADMITTING THE THINGS THAT
WE REALLY WANT. SAYING YES TO THEM. KNOWING
WHAT WE DON'T WANT AND SAYING NO. NO MORE. NO
WAY. NAVIGATING GRIEF. GRATITUDE AS AN EXERCISE.

The Swing of Things

Somewhere, somehow,

we have grown afraid. Again.

But nothing is lost. We'll return

(we have done this before, of course).

To be human is to remember and forget,

and repeat.

REMEMBER FORGET REMEMBER FORGET REMEMBER

FORGET REMEMBER FORGET REMEMBER FORGET

REMEMBER FORGET REMEMBER FORGET REMEMBER

FORGET REMEMBER FORGET REMEMBER FORGET

REMEMBER FORGET REMEMBER FORGET REMEMBER

FORGET REMEMBER FORGET REMEMBER FORGET

REMEMBER FORGET REMEMBER FORGET REMEMBER

All Our Best Lessons Are Circles

on remembering

There is a calm knowing in your being, a gentle understanding sitting in the core of each of us. It is a deeply experienced part of you, one that knows your desire. This is why each fresh discovery still bears a whiff of the familiar. As though, somehow, you have already been here. As though, somehow, you are remembering.

How funny that we always presume we are the first generation to have invented a feeling. How self-centered we are, believing our forebears knew less of boredom and anxiety. Sometimes your grandma was bored too. Sometimes she did not think she could face the next day. Often, she was nervous about the future. If you feel it, she has felt it. There are no new core states of being. Restlessness, dissatisfaction, and Fear Of Missing Out are as old as time. We felt them in 740 and we felt them in 1548 and we will feel them in 2085, provided we are not kicked off our long-suffering planet. We will still wonder if we are artists or creatives or frauds, if we are enough, if we are losing our minds. We will wonder why we do not have work or why we do not like our work or why we are not making work, or we will worry if the work we are making is good enough. We will still worry about love. We will worry about making love, or if the love that we make is good enough. The truth is, we will always worry.

I worry that in writing this book, nothing much will change in my life. It's quite true. Nothing much will. In my heart of hearts, I know that I can never look to anything external as a way out of myself, though this knowledge does not stop me from trying. The book will be done, and I will be thinking or not thinking about another. I will worry about several other things in my life and I will repeat. Life is so very cyclical that the ending can never be the answer. It is only ever a mirage, some imagined place, a trick of the light. When one issue feels resolved, does not another require your attention, almost immediately? Do not several concerns flood across our minds all at once, competing for space and energy? If it were not so, no one would have to keep working. You would have gone to work once or twice and learned a thing or two, and that would be enough.

So, what is the point of the constant circle? What is the point of striving for anything if what we are really looking for will never complete itself?

If only we could remember: we were small and full once, and the sky was wide open. Whether our situation was ideal or not, we could still imagine something else, and we did so with ease. This imagining was not a burden—it was the point. But as we grew, so did our doubts. Now that we are older, we tend to focus on the limitations of a situation. Whichever way we look at it, our focus remains on the box of the circumstance: the shrinking dimensions, the constraints, all the things that seem to be up against us. Because we are so used to thinking in this way, even when we get the things that we think we want, we quickly find that they are:

1. not really the things we wanted

2. not nearly as good as we imagined

3. what we wanted, but now we want something else

Or/and

4. almost as good as we imagined, but not for long

But there is a way out of this predicament, a route to a wide-open sky.

How to start?

Think of two things that you want—two large and perfect scenarios—invoking as much detail as you can, suspending any disbelief that they might not happen. In short, do not start thinking about how improbable they are. Write them down. Focus on each of them for twenty seconds each. (Twenty seconds is much longer than it seems.) Imagine details about them and how they might feel.

Imagining can feel impractical, but that is exactly why it works. It does not have to make sense. You do not need to worry about *how*. We are not so weighed down with effort when we engage our imaginations; rather, we are free, boundless and light. The trick to this exercise is not your focus on the lack of the thing but ultimate belief in the thing itself, and what feeling is created in the body when you let yourself fall into it. If you are new to this, it may take some tries . . . and you may not be able to synthesize a feeling of excitement right away or for very long. Keep trying. When your body starts to change, pay attention to where that feeling occurs. Locate this new stirring in the body. Hold on to the feeling for as long as possible, before your thoughts drift.

There are many intertwining levels on which this practice works. You will attract more things into your life by subconsciously creating conditions where they can arrive. This happens because you set yourself up to receive. Your body will locate, synthesize, produce a good feeling, and therefore register how it wants to feel. We shift our expectations and clear receiving space in our body, thus priming the body to understand and recognize what a certain kind of joy feels like. Once we know it, and know that we want it, we'll attract even more of it. You do yourself a service every time you allow yourself this feeling. Not to mention that it's a good exercise for your imagination. It is great for your chemistry too, since your body cannot tell the difference between a real or imagined experience. The more you let this happen in your body, the more you will pull similar things toward you, giving you the same result again and again: pure, unadulterated shots of delight.

First, you dream. Make it up as you go along. Think large and wild, and focus on how you want it to feel, above all other details and thoughts. Get as specific as you can about the feeling. You will continue to attract more and more experiences which bring it about.

Milestones and Other Cons

destination versus now

We are here for a prescribed and brief amount of time, a blip, longer for some than others. We are here to create, to love, to learn, to grow, to share our gifts, and, very importantly, to experience *joy*. It's not about getting to point B but "the journey," they say—and it sounds like a lie. But it is truer than we realize. What is point B anyway but number two in a long list of *even more things*?

To be clear, when I speak of joy, I do not mean the intangible state that we call *happiness*. When I speak of joy, I speak of something altogether more nuanced and real to me; something I can taste and feel and name. I speak of the experience and dynamism of being alive in the world. I speak of darkness and light, arousal and feeling. Joy is largely to be found in the dreaming and conceiving of a thing, the traveling toward it, who we are when we are with others in or around our path, and what we do on the way.

The destination is no fixed point, and it is never all it is promised to be. No sooner do we land than we look for the very next place on which to set our sights. That in itself is no bad thing. It is incredible (and natural) that our desires are always regenerating, that our desires should shift. But we should be wary of assigning a feeling of ultimate satisfaction to the experience of completion, or we will be disappointed. In order to feel vital and have any real enjoyment, we must find the beauty in the dreaming and planning and less so in the outcome. If joy is to exist at all, it can only ever be *now*. Otherwise, nothing great is solved when we succeed. We think that there will be this fanfare and happiness will come. But no. If you do not feel joy in the getting it, there'll be no more joy in the having it. Sorry. Humans are just set up that way. We love a problem to solve, a thing to make our God, something we can exalt, something to pin our dreams on. Nothing will *give* you "the feeling." It must exist on its own, without condition. Alive and breathing, reliant on nothing.

This does not always seem to make sense, since validation, whether social or monetary, seems to lie on the other side of the line, the green over yonder, the next place. When we have achieved [INSERT MILESTONE], things will be better. When you have gone [INSERT PLACE], things will be better. When you have acquired [INSERT NEW MATERIAL THING], things will be better. This is because we live in a system that applauds material wealth, appearances, and status. But even after gaining some of the things that we said we wanted, we are still never quite there.

Well, what is the point of the journey, you might say, if our day in the sun means nothing? If the accolades and achievements are pointless?

I do not mean to deny the importance of goals. As highlighted in the previous chapter, it is a transformative exercise to name and say what we want, and to imagine those things with creativity and delight. But I speak to the intentionality of the goal: what we want, and for what reasons. I mean that the goal will solve nothing, in and of itself, if we are not suitably equipped. I mean that we can't use the promise and gifts of tomorrow to escape this very moment. If you are not spiritually fit right now, running anywhere else is pointless. The next place will never save you.

Name four things that you wanted and now have.
Do you still want them? Did they change you? For how long?

Name four things that you attach great value to now.
How long have you wanted them? Is there anything that links them together?
Do you think that they will change you? If so, how?

Now, think of two instances in which you are completely fixed on some future outcome. How can you actively begin to enjoy your progress toward those goals in *this* very moment?

Such inquiries are important, whether we know the answers right away or the questions hang in the background, flowering.

If We Were Different,
We'd Be Perfect

what to do with all the noise

Can you hear your thoughts clearly today? Are you breathing as deeply as you might? Do you feel alert? Energized? Connected to the bones of yourself? I ask because these times are testing, and many are seeking The How. We are in a constant state of trying to improve, to maintain, to cope, to stay ahead. And we are living in a brash, incessant economy where everything is competing for our attention. Sales. Precautions. New information. Warnings. There are countless messages coming from everywhere, all of them urging us to be different than we are. The messages are infinite. So much work goes into each one of these commands too, and together they create a low-level and overall hum of not-quite-thereness. They are coaxing you out of yourself, promising you the world if you will only agree and conform. We all know better, and at the same time, we don't. Even if we have gotten better at not listening to the machine, the noise continues on in the background. When we try to ignore the messages, they seep into the meat of us and settle in our bones. As such, we take them on, whether we rebel or comply, whether we mean to or not.

Sometimes it is pressure to join a culture, group, or political leaning. What if your feelings do not align with theirs? What if they don't truly resonate? You swallow it down. You grow withdrawn, insecure. Sometimes it happens within your religion, when you judge yourself against its teachings and feel less than "good." Sometimes it is the loud and constant pressure to look different than you do. Sometimes the comparison is not so obvious or conscious, but it happens, slowly and surely, weathering you on the inside. You see someone's social media feed and you keep score on how much they seem to be excelling. Now you think twice about what you are eating, or what you are wearing, or if you should be talking about the thing that everyone's talking about, or whether the relationship you're in is really the best you can get. Sometimes the coaxing is a call to action or politics. Sometimes it is a new, expensive thing that must be acquired. Sometimes it's a thing to help you live longer, at least in theory. It is a persistent, insidious ache, so dull and so common, appearing in any direction we turn.

And we are bewildered. If we drink as much water and exercise as often and eat green and as fresh as we should
and if we water our plants and check our teeth, breasts, and testicles
and if we look after our money and stay on top of our taxes

and if I write out all of the ideas that are in my head and keep my eyelashes long and my hair soft and stay in contact with my family who need me and pay it forward and mentor and meditate and learn to do handstands and backbends and other yogic feats,

if you and I try to do all the things we are told to do to be the very best that we can be, then we will never rest.

If I choose to produce as much written work as I can and honor every single deadline without fail and remember to optimize everything, I will be doing so much less of the other stuff. Forget learning a new language. Forget fun. Forget travel. Forget a good sex life or any sex at all. Forget deepening a relationship with the people around me. Forget forging new ones. Unless we learn to multitask or forgo several "important things," we will constantly feel bereft. We will feel not good enough. We will feel as though everyone has it figured out but us, and we will mourn the many things we cannot do.

What if what feels important to us is also a distortion? What if most of these things only *seem* important because of what we have been conditioned to believe?

Since days are not infinite in the world we have created, we will have to become ruthless about removing the things that do not feel worth it, activities that that waste the hours, leaving us with little in return. In order to feel better, we should feel as though the things that we are doing are truly important to us. We must pay attention to what adds meaning to our life and what steals from it. We have to choose. And then we must prioritize this growing mass, as regularly and thoroughly as we can. Only then will we uncover more time, more velocity, more *life*.

This sounds easier than it is. How can we be sure of the things we are here to do and the things we can leave behind? How do we let go of the wills and expectations of others? This is extremely important, particularly if you find yourself easily influenced by the urges of others and especially if you deal with unwarranted feelings of guilt. You have to reduce the noise in order to hear yourself. That means fewer hours scrolling on social media. Less television. Less exposure to advertisements. Less mindless consumption of media, social and otherwise. Less gossip, complaining, and collective outrage. Less small talk. Mark out any period of time (from a week to a few months) when you decide that the answer to everything that is not an absolute *yes* is a clear and definite *no*.

When you are next in a quiet room, think of five things that you do not want to do that you somehow still feel obliged to do.

In the quiet of the room you are in, practice saying no; see how it feels in the mouth. Play with the texture of the word. Draw it out. Sing it out the dark. Watch it settle in the air. Let out as any many of them as you like. Let it come, loud, and ragged and low as you like. Do not control it, and do not qualify, just say it out loud, and mean it.

NO NO NO NO NO NO NO NO NO NO NO NO NO NO NO NO NO
NO NO NO NO NO NO NO NO NO NO NO NO NO NO NO NO NO
NO NO NO NO NO NO NO NO NO NO NO NO NO NO NO NO NO
NO NO NO NO NO NO NO NO NO NO NO NO NO NO NO NO NO
NO NO NO NO NO NO NO NO NO NO NO NO NO NO NO NO NO
NO NO NO NO NO NO NO NO NO NO NO NO NO NO NO NO NO
NO NO NO NO NO NO NO NO NO NO NO NO NO NO NO NO NO
NO NO NO NO NO NO NO NO NO NO NO NO NO NO NO NO NO
NO NO NO NO NO NO NO NO NO NO NO NO NO NO NO NO NO
NO NO NO NO NO NO NO NO NO NO NO NO NO NO NO NO NO
NO NO NO NO NO NO NO NO NO NO NO NO NO NO NO NO NO
NO NO NO NO NO NO NO NO NO NO NO NO NO NO NO NO NO
NO NO NO NO NO NO NO NO NO NO NO NO NO NO NO NO NO
NO NO NO NO NO NO NO NO NO NO NO NO NO NO NO NO NO
NO NO NO NO NO NO NO NO NO NO NO NO NO NO NO NO NO

Set the alarm on your phone to go off at least three times over the weekend. Pause when it does and take a moment to write about what you are doing in that exact moment, and why.

What messages might you have absorbed that motivated this action?

Do they align with the things that are important to you? Do they align with the things that bring the most joy or peace?

If yes, how? If no, why? How might you begin to disrupt these patterns?

YOU ARE MORE THAN YOUR BODY. YOUR FEARS. YOUR PRODUCTIVITY. YOUR YEARS ON THE PLANET. THE FIGURES IN YOUR BANK. WHAT THEY CALL ACHIEVEMENTS. THE THINGS YOU HAVE FINISHED. THE THINGS YOU HAVE NOT FINISHED. WHAT YOU CAN SEE. WHAT YOU ARE TALKING ABOUT. WHAT YOU ARE SAYING ABOUT YOURSELF. WHAT IS SAID ABOUT YOU. WHERE YOU ARE. YOUR PLANS. HOW MUCH YOU EAT OR DO NOT EAT. HOW MUCH YOU DRINK OR DO NOT DRINK. THE PLACE WHERE YOU LEARNED. WHO YOU SLEPT WITH OR DID NOT SLEEP WITH. WHAT THEY CALL YOUR LOOKS. YOUR HUNGER. YOUR SEX DRIVE. THE BOOKS YOU HAVE READ. WHERE YOU HAVE BEEN OR HAVE NOT BEEN. YOUR PHYSICAL STRENGTH. WHERE YOU ARE, RIGHT NOW. WHAT THEY CALL SUCCESS. WHAT YOU SPEND OR DO NOT SPEND. WHO AND WHAT YOU LOVE.

Outside In

discovering the message

You get up. You move your body.

You move your body and open the door.

You open the door, and outside, everything is alive in performance. A low, sustained hum surrounds you, as though the earth were holding you in a song. Is the earth holding you in a song?

There is something new about the trees today. But there is always something new and old about the trees. Each one is different to its neighbor, and the range of greens filters messages down to the street life below.

You are the street life, and you can be part of this circle of growing, seasoning things, if you choose. The movement is happening around you whether you understand it or not. (Mostly, we do not understand.)

High above you, those trees stand and bend toward and away from each other, attentive, certain. If you listen and hold still enough to be part of the conversation, you will be all the more informed. There is much treasure to be gained from surrendering to the hum of your surroundings. It can bring you back to yourself, and beyond, into the other lives that are possible, and beckoning.

Do you remember when you were little and they told you to put a seashell to your ear? They told you that you could hear the ocean, and then when you got older, you decided, No. That's the sea in me. Those are the rough waves in me.
How did I not know my own blood?

Your environment has this way of showing you yourself by showing you *itself*: reflecting back your own points of darkness and light. Every self has its own unique drum pattern. Do you remember the things that you want? What do you think your soul is asking you for? You have to be still to hear the message. You have to be still to be inspired to do something about it. You have to be still to know how to move. Sometimes the doing is in doing nothing. Does this make sense to you? I would be happy to start again. We can always begin again, and that is the beauty.

Outside, the world around you booms, alive with activity. Even if the activity is perfect calm. Some days you think that you missed the messages from the earth, because you did not go out, because you did not open a door or a window, or yourself. Or maybe you did, but you rushed and were concerned with immediate, painful things. Know that you did not miss the messages. Nature saves them for you. It saves them in your body.

Our bodies know the truth about us. The fluid, cells, and gristle that make us up tally our excitements, pain, love, and trauma. Think of numbness, of ringing in the ears, of hot flashes on the sudden remembrance of a thing or pain when you don't, but you do, but you don't.

This truth-keeping is often the reason why spiky darts of fear will turn our legs unsteady or make us feel faint, or why sometimes a deep feeling of unease will find us when we didn't see it coming, or why something like fatigue will suddenly sweep the body when we think of the things we have to do and none of them are anything that we *want* to do. It can be the reason that the blood cells cease to function. How do we not know our own blood?

You remember the lyrics to the songs of your childhood.
You remember the first and second names of the popular kids at school. You remember your last few addresses or
you remember how the kiss felt, or the small humiliations that still make you squirm to this day.
You still feel hot over some past injustice.
Yet we continue to underestimate how much information is stored in the body. How much is locked away, forever working for or against our momentum.

I did not think to ask why I was afraid of large dogs. I accepted it as a natural fear I had from birth. Early last year, my older brother let me know that I was charged by two large dogs when I was tiny and that I howled and shook for hours, entirely traumatized. He went on to tell me that later the very same day, my mum totaled the car in a serious car crash, and it was a wonder that we survived, unhurt. I consciously remember none of this, although my body does. Of course it does. For years I have been re-creating my own fear about a whole host of things. Dogs. Swimming. Rejection. Poverty. Without ever knowing it, I kept them alive.

Today I rarely come clean about my latent fear of dogs. Well, what is the point? The idea of the fear is fading, and I observe it and smile every time a dog comes running toward me. My breathing might change as I touch the animal, some involuntary twitch, a tiny remnant of something almost forgotten in the mind, an echo of which reverberates in my body. But the truth is shifting. Each time that I pet a dog and breathe through the motion, I am rewriting myself in a small way. Sometimes, if I remember to, I feel at peace.

You can start again. Outside or indoors, find somewhere where you can be still and undistracted. Even if you cannot hear your heart, you can feel your breath, and that is all you need.

You listen. To nothing at first.

You listen to nothing until it slowly becomes *something*. It might be a sensation or a wish, or a feeling, or a vision. It may not happen the first day, but it will happen. If you open up the pathways, inspiration has no choice but to seep into you from the heavens and the depths. You allow yourself to become a vessel by staying as connected to your source as possible. By opening up the channel, by listening, with intent.

Perhaps you really want to work on yourself, but you have all of these questions locked in your body. You want to have more courage to change, but your fear of the unknown cramps you. You want to stand up for yourself or someone else, but you have all these examples, all of this human-made evidence, of why you are not worthy. You worry what people will say when you show them the truth about you. Your body wants to do new and unfamiliar things. You want to come pouring out of yourself.

It can happen, and it will. It takes less effort than you are using. Breathe now. Be right here, now. Turn your face to the sky, which has always shown up for you. For a few seconds, turn off your mind.

When you see the natural, bright colors of a bird,
when you see the shock of a branch bursting into flower,
when you see the sun reflected on the face of a glittering, high building, you must recognize each miracle as part of your existence, memory, story—as something you belong to. There are some days, many of them, when we are apt to forget this. We are human, and often we think of ourselves as lone, separate entities, forgetting that we are connected to this odd and expanding universe, forgetting that we are part of something vast and unexplained. Something strange. Something larger than life.

The next time you can, go outside and find an ensemble of trees. Stand underneath the knowledge, the expanse, the just-so-ness of nature.

Breathe in time with the nature you are looking at, concentrating on only the sound of your surroundings. Every time another thought comes into your head, respond with breath, turning your attention back to your source, back to nothing else but the sounds of the outdoors.

Breathe deeply, with as clear a mind as you can muster, with no other intention than simply being, belonging completely to this moment. This moment is here only once.

You are as brilliant as the best thing in nature and could only be here because you belong here, wild and unpredictable as everything else.

Let's Talk About the Water

on movement and fluidity

You move because you must, yes?

You move toward a river, a lake, or the sea. You peer down, observing the way the water ripples and refracts the great light above, the way it converses cleanly with air and sky. You find yourself close to the edge of a universe, older and larger than all of us. Water holds all the truth in the world. And yet it changes shape and color, adapts from form to form, shifts, freezes, warms, sizzles, evaporates into the atmosphere. Water consistently adapts to survive, and so must we, being all made up of it. Salt water and blood and elements of sky.

When we were children, we mastered our language by mimicking what we were shown. As soon as we were too old for a thing, we moved on (and were quick to announce the fact). We were tumbling and wild. We couldn't wait to get older.

Well, look at us. We got older, didn't we? We stiffened, grew fixed and frighteningly sure of what we were. And in turn, we reached an age where nobody could tell us anything new about ourselves. We made up all of our stories, constructing them around us like nests. And for a lot of us, this is where we remain, safe and hidden, hiding from other possible truths.

We do more damage than we realize by repeating these old, irrelevant narratives. We allow long-ago plotlines and descriptions that are no longer relevant to define us and set deeper into our bones as fact. We allow them to impair our movement and vision. But the only true, sure thing is impermanence: growth, changes, the unknown.

Observe the water meeting the sky (and it always will). Water respects no bounds, stays out of nowhere. Water will flow into every space it is allowed to, wetting the very farthest untouched places. Stray into the new spaces and places that you have imagined and allow yourself the courage to continually adjust. That is the essence of the stream itself. We cannot grow if we resist changing shape.

It is arrogant of me to presume that I know precisely what I am and that *what I am* will never change. It is impossible to be right here, right now, while still overidentifying with a self-imposed label, something in my past. It is impossible for me to be entirely in the now while existing as I always have. In adopting a fixed attitude, I do myself a disservice. The effort I use to call myself "terrible with names," "a procrastinator," or "accident prone" would be much better placed in crafting and flowing, resistance-free, into something new.

Why are we so set on limiting ourselves? There is little to no effort involved in a state of flow. All the forces work with you. This is the reason why affirmations are so powerful and effective: you repeat and repeat something useful until it becomes bloodline. You fall into them with trust and ease. You fall into them because, often, without even knowing it, you are retelling your own story. You are crafting an entirely new experience.

Be intentional with the story you are designing. You are your life's work.

When you talk about yourself, watch your language. If something no longer feels right, if there is a mode of being and thinking that no longer serves, if you suspect that you may have shifted into another phase, stay open. Pour out what has become muddied or stagnant and be eager and ruthless about it. This is your life, so begin it today, without apology. The thing about being a living, breathing part of nature is that you are never the same twice.

Water shifts, allows itself to be added unto, turned over, thrown against the wall. And water smashes itself against the wall with all of its might. It learns something new every minute. It cleanses itself by creating more of itself.

It is not about knowing what to do. My god, who knows what to do? Part of the joy is that we don't know. Most of the experience is learning. It is about being fluid and malleable, and open and wide.

Just be more you: that's the solution. By being receptive, by gently shifting, we become even more of what we are. Always be new in some small way. That is the liquid of life, well lived. You filter by collecting yourself, stretching out, breathing new life into all your parts, willing them health, and flushing out what no longer works. We should always be letting go.

Is there an old story flying around about you from the past? Are you the author? Are you still telling the same tale on yourself? Is it a low, outdated tale? Do you cling to an identity that is working against you? Write down the things that you are clinging to in the name of *identity*.

When you lie in bed tonight, or next go for a long walk, consider a new story.

Even the smallest shift helps. When we allow new water, new salt, to be formed around a new skill, a new desire, it is a welcome injection. Think of three core things you think you are not good at or skills you know you don't have. Aim to look into each of them this month. New water. Have the conversation you have been avoiding. New water. Take active and firm hold of a relationship that no longer serves you and call it what it is. New water.

It is not about an instant dramatic change; it is about looking. It is about taking stock—whether something is still a part of you or whether you are made up of something else these days. Water constantly opens itself up to more, more, more, and infinity. You have always been mostly water. You attract newness as naturally as you breathe.

I NEED AND DESERVE NEWNESS. I AM ALLOWING MORE OF MYSELF EACH MOMENT. I WELCOME NEW OPPORTUNITIES, NEW DESIRES. I ALLOW WHAT I ONCE WANTED TO EVAPORATE INTO AIR, AND INTO SKY. I SMILE AT WISHES ONCE CAST, ONCE BELOVED, ONCE IMPORTANT. I AM SOFTLY AWARE OF THE OLD PATHWAYS MY MIND CREATED, KNOWING THEY NO LONGER SERVE MY EMERGING PURPOSE. IT IS TIME FOR THEM TO SHIFT, MAKING WAY FOR THE NEW TRUTHS. I TRUST THE INTUITION RUNNING THROUGH ME, THAT DIVINE AND INEFFABLE SPARK. I DESERVE AND WELCOME CHANGE AFTER CHANGE, THE WASHING AWAY OF FADING FACTS. I'M A LOUD AND GENTLE LIGHT, AND WILL BE SO LONG AS I'M HERE. WHETHER FEARFUL OR NOT, I MOVE BECAUSE I MUST.

The God of the Rainbow

showing up and understanding purpose

In a story that plays out to me again and again,

there lives this great god of the sea and sky. The god is bright and powerful and specializes in the rainbow and its stunning transmissions. Each time the heavens open and close, the rainbow appears, and the god arches themselves beautifully across the entire sky, at the exact middle point between the heavens and the earth. The thing (and there is always a thing) is that the god of the sea and sky worries about their purpose and worthiness. The god of the sea and sky constantly worries about this. Often, when they have finished their work of becoming the rainbow, there is silence and a feeling of calm in the world. The god misunderstands this, taking the silence for indifference. They do not think the rainbow is needed, because the world cannot tell them so. If only the god could see how their work makes the earth thrive, how the rainbow is reproduced in countless artworks, how rainbows are depicted in poems, stories, and film, how children and adults alike enjoy them, things might be different. But they are arched upward and out, and their eyes are always pointing the opposite way. Up toward the sky, questioning everything. (Even gods have earthly desires and miss matters of great importance.)

Eventually, the god of the rainbow loses their joy in the work. They hide themselves away. They feel like an impostor now: unworthy, incomplete,

as though they have already lost too much. All their colors are still there for anyone to see, but the longer they hide from the sun, the duller they feel. One day their colors simply aren't there. Or they are

(of course they are)

but the truth doesn't matter. The truth is always changing and becoming what we make it.

Anyway, another god replaces them, and they are relieved, and go off to hide in the mountains to do other things. Over the years that follow, they become transparent and turn into the mist you see around the mountains. They never lose their power; they just stop using it.

Of course, the god is you and the god is me and the god is our parents, and this is almost a tragedy, but not quite, not yet. After all, we are still here.

Think of three instances in which your existence is making a difference in someone else's life. Think of three instances in which someone else is making a difference in your own life, even if the benefit is not entirely obvious (for example, they are showing you what you don't want).

Your existence alone is a one-in-a-million result of excellent work, negotiation, and perfect timing. Showing up is work, and offers more inspiration and importance to those around you than you will ever understand. Know this, even if no one ever tells you.

Save Yourself

on the growing need for selfishness

It gets exhausting, forever chasing The How. We find ourselves repeatedly fired up by some new idea, practice, or solution, only to lose the will and fast plummet. We have plenty of distractions working sharply away at our undersides, forever gnawing at the edges of things—a constant slew of muddy information: lurking and precious and common and awful and terrible and gorgeous and urgent and frightening and pressing and depressing and shallow and too deep for comfort and chiding and aching and telling you what you are and telling you what you aren't and putting you in your place and desperate and unnecessary and good and nonsense and all of it much too much.

So you sit at home, tepid and folding, in the middle of the day. You tell yourself that no one else is doing this. Most other people have lives or loves, or a job they (at least) show up for. The good ones are doing something more immediate—winning— and they're better than you. You are overloaded. You do not know where to start. You feel like you are disappointing everyone, most of all yourself.

How do you get over this?

You have to save yourself and worry about the rest later.

Perhaps this sounds like selfishness. You are invited to be selfish. You will not be free if you do not take deep, profound care of your soul, your body, your spirit. Leave this out and you can only ever be a fraction of yourself. Before you save a single thing, you must first save yourself. It is a revolutionary act, and every revolution must begin in the heart.

Those who do not feel low, unmotivated, or stuck these days are most likely this way because they have tried-and-tested systems in place. They plan, or they believe, or they simply know what works. They gaze at the gentle morning sun, and fill up their bodies lovingly, and choose their own stories, and hold close ones close. For them, The How has become a solid practice or religion. They know that there is now little choice but to keep what works and throw away what doesn't. They know that giving thanks for even the smallest things that you treasure will attract even more of these things. They know that when they are feeling below par, it is likely because they have veered from the checklist of things that keep them balanced. And what of that checklist? How did they begin to understand, to create what worked for them? How did they draw up a system to follow? How did they identify their own nonnegotiables?

They invested in themselves by giving new practices a try. Even if they initially disbelieved, even if they were starting from little to no knowledge at all, they humored themselves and began.

Begin. Try something else. The life force in you is willing you to go on winning. Know that you are already prevailing, because you are here. Even when you don't feel like being here.

Your cells, your veins, your capillaries, your bones, your blessed organs—they are stacked in your favor, they would like you to win; if they did not, you would not have made it this far. You are excellent metal. Startling machinery. Your body, pure genius. Even your hairs grow on their own; you do not tell them to. There are things happening all the time that you are mostly unaware of; your brain the conductor, your body in constant concert. And what can we say about the thoughts that go ringing down your limbs unnoticed?

If you are tired (and you might indeed be tired),
remember the multiple moving parts that hold you up
without asking you to show them how.
It took a miracle to make you in the first place,
and from hour to hour, you go on being made.

Here you are, ever-changing, gathering color. Here you are, ripening. A harvester of ideas. A container for unlit potential. Here you are, red cells working, new blood being made, and a heart that won't turn off just yet. There are lucky miracles happening at the top of your body, gently waiting to be released at dream time, when you're safely out of the way.

Here is a single prescription: allow yourself beauty. We must fill the days with lifelines and rewards; we must mine the splendor of everything. We must become purveyors of small beauties, things to return to every day, comforting, sure things. Even while the ground is unsteady, we must be able to hold on to something real, something touchable.

If you take an early morning walk, try to notice three new, pleasing things. If you call someone who needs something that you can help them with cheerfully, do it with as much pleasure as you can. When you drink water, feel the sensation and relief in every gulp, the wetness in your mouth. When you eat, eat deliberately, paying deep attention to flavor, taste, and texture. Each time you enjoy something, you have an experience that will never be exactly the same ever again. Dazzling things go unnoticed by us all day, every day.

Before you save the world, save yourself, since you are the only one capable of this. You are the only one able to oil the machine magic, enabling it to operate at its highest potential. *To save your life, parts of you have to die. Let them com-*

bust into a thousand more useful things. Learn the behaviors that keep you up and running and those that keep you down.

Make an inventory of everything that you do that works for you, a clear and precise inventory of nonnegotiables. Is it exercise that keeps you energized and loose? Is it deep breathing that keeps your mind sharp? Is it family that keeps you thankful? Is it prayer that keeps you calm? Nature? Time connecting with animals? Playing sports? What are the core ingredients that work for you? When you have made a list, turn it around. Now make a note of the habits, things, and people that leave you feeling *less* energized.

As I write, I am thinking about currency, about attention, about power, and how I must fill myself adequately before I can share with any other. And as I write, I consider the millions of directions my mind has twisted itself into even in the course of the last hour and the droplets of thought that were blooming and useful and the droplets of thought that hit the floor and vanished, never to be found again. Yes, I must save myself and, yes, you must save yourself. "Selfish" has horrible press, and yet this inward focus, this business of feeling good, is vital when it comes to wealth of the mind. To live well, your mind must be a fruitful place with much peace and permission to rest. To live well, you have to *want* to live.

When we are tired (and we are indeed tired),
we need new ways.

The War, the Bloody War

on depression

Sometimes, while not particularly thinking about one thing or the other, you sense the thing that lurks. Before it has even revealed itself, you feel it on its way to you. It is a certain dappled gray, with murky, unspecific contents. Perhaps it creeps toward you in the mornings or late at night. It lies in wait until you are tired and at your most susceptible. By night you feel shaken, as though somehow a small hole has appeared in your covering, allowing doubt to creep in. Gone is the light optimism of the morning, and you begin creating small and specific ways to feel worse about yourself. The heaviness is vast and unrelenting in its act. It has myriad faces. It manifests as stress, pain, fatigue, depression. It causes you to lose track of the present; a particularly sharp kind of sabotage. When we are overtaken by the thing that lurks, we lose out on *now*. We strip ourselves of our most vital autonomy when we are spiraling, worrying, about what has happened in the past and what might happen in our future, instead of what is here, right now. In those moments, when we are vulnerable to the large and overwhelming forces in our midst, the sure antidote is to bring ourselves into this present as much as we can. Despite what we are told, there is no better time to be in than right now.

Now.

Do it now. Now is the time. Be awake and in touch with it, because *now* regenerates in an instant. It is all we have, shapeshifting before our eyes, coming and going away and appearing. It is gone in a moment and around forever. If this paradox will not alert you to the ferocity and significance of the time you are in, what will?

Now is when you wake up and decide what the day will be, and now is the dream itself, ebbing away with every waking second, and now is the residue, what you planned for and what you didn't plan for, and none of it matters anyway because here we are. Now is a result of everything we thought we knew.

"Do it now" does not mean springing headfirst into action. It means being present; listening for the signs, so that you are able to respond intuitively to the beat, to blossoming thoughts and ideas. Now is the time for you to catch up to them. Now is always the time. Do not second-guess yourself, or this moment, by waiting for another. Do not ignore the beauty of the day in favor of some perfect, imagined future. Now has always belonged to you, and it will, as long as you live.

You catch up with yourself by being in the present. When you are next in a space of your own, notice the small things that make up the room. Study them, paying specific attention to the objects that you usually overlook. Consider each item, its story, what it means to you. What is the overall feeling that each item inspires in you? One by one, make a case for as many items as you have time to consider. Do you still have use for it now? Does it still deserve space in your immediate environment?

DO IT NOW. FOR SOME INSTANT RELIEF, BREATHE SLOWLY, DEEPLY. LOOK UP TO THE SKY. PAUSE THERE FOR TEN SECONDS, NO MATTER WHAT YOU ARE FEELING. SEE IF THE FEELING CHANGES; SEE WHAT IT IS THAT CHANGES (SOMETHING WILL CHANGE). LOVE THE BODY BY STRETCHING GENTLY AND WITH INTENTION. DRINK WATER. SING THE OLDEST SONG YOU REMEMBER. LISTEN TO A PIECE OF GREAT MUSIC. BE A FRIEND TO YOUR WONDER-FILLED BODY. DANCE. CALL SOMEONE YOU WANT TO SPEAK TO. SPEND TIME WITH A CHILD. PICK UP THINGS THAT ARE LYING ON THE FLOOR. WRITE DOWN YOUR THOUGHTS. WASH. LIGHT A CANDLE. SWEEP THE FLOOR. LISTEN TO SOME HIGH-VIBRATIONAL MUSIC. REST YOUR EYES. TOUCH YOUR BODY. MAKE A TO-DO LIST. MAKE A PLAYLIST. WRITE A BEAUTIFUL LETTER TO SOMEONE. TELL SOMEONE WHY YOU LOVE THEM. MAKE A GIFT. MEDITATE. HUM. DANCE SOME MORE. PRAY TO WHATEVER OR WHOMEVER YOU PRAY TO. MAKE A GRATITUDE LIST. ORGANIZE A SMALL, BELOVED SECTION OF YOUR SPACE. TELL SOMEONE THAT YOU ARE MOVING ON, AND DO NOT BE SORRY ABOUT IT. THANK SOMEONE FOR SOMETHING. WIPE

DOWN YOUR SURFACES LOVINGLY AND WITH INTENT. EXPERIMENT WITH COLOR. WATCH AN EPISODE OF A TV SHOW YOU LOVE. DRAW. INSTALL A TIME-REDUCTION APP ACROSS YOUR DEVICES. HAND-WASH YOUR DELICATES, PAYING DEEP ATTENTION TO THE ACTION IN HAND. WRITE ANYTHING YOU CALL A POEM. RECYCLE CLOTHES AND ALL OTHER ITEMS THAT YOU DO NOT LOVE. GET RID OF THINGS THAT REMIND YOU OF NOT BEING EXACTLY WHERE YOU WANT TO BE. THROW OUT OR RECYCLE ITEMS THAT ARE PAST THEIR BEST. EXPLORE A NEW SKILL, RIGHT FROM THE VERY BEGINNING. OFFER YOUR SERVICES TO SOMEONE WHO IS OLDER. ASK SOMEONE YOUNGER HOW YOU MIGHT ASSIST THEM. ORGANIZE THREE CHEAP AND SIMPLE THINGS THAT WILL MAKE YOUR LIFE FLOW WITH MORE EASE. NAP. MAKE LOVE. IF YOU LIKE YOUR FAMILY, ARRANGE A GET-TOGETHER; IF YOU DO NOT LIKE YOUR FAMILY, ARRANGE A GET-TOGETHER WITH PEOPLE YOU LIKE. GO OUT ALONE INTO WILD, SOOTHING NATURE. DO IT NOW.

Site Beauty

the magic of specificity

Even in times like now, with all our technology and distractions, there is no experience like wandering through a green space after it has rained, particularly all night or through the morning hours, and being overcome with its sweet, insistent aroma. There is a distinct art to watching and being, noticing with or without comment the outstretched palm of a leaf, how softly the trees kiss the ground. Always, we learn the largest acts of love from nature. How it shows up in its cycles. How it provides a backdrop for the dramas of our lives to occur. How it shows us itself again and again and asks us for nothing.

But often, all caught up in what there is to do and to think and repeat, we miss the outrageous beauty of the scene. We're much more concerned with letting the prerecorded narratives of our old lives play over and over again, and with responding to what has happened, and all the things that we think we know. There's nothing new to see when we repeat this pattern, but we do it anyway—such is the nature of our mutual, terrible habit.

When you are moving outdoors, try to spend some moments where you allow everything to occur to you as if by magic and chance. To notice is to fall in love with the gifts of the everyday, over and over again. To *notice* is to open up and allow things to become part of your experience. It clears the clutter from the mind, allows space for the new. The next time you leave the house, or gaze out of a window, consider the following:

What do I notice? What are the elements that call out to me? How do they appeal to my senses? What do they remind me of?

This dance with nature is a love affair. Our bodies were intended to work alongside the earth, nourishing it as it nourishes us. It is no coincidence that the very air we breathe is given to us by plants and the very air that we expel is taken in by plants. Did we maneuver or stress or organize to ensure these happenings? We did not. And it is no coincidence that those same plants are the ones with which we fill our bodies. Did we plan any of this? We did not.

We cut ourselves off from these sacred happenings each time we believe that it is our self-willed action that ensures our security on this planet. Furthermore, thinking like this will leave us sadly unconscious of everything else at play. The wonder of nature goes on and on, with us and without us. It is unstoppable and measureless, and we are so caught up in our own heads most of the time that we miss it. We are missing so much every time we behave as though the world is something outside of ourselves. We turn our attention instead to what is not working out for us, what does not seem to love us, what does not seem to give us anything back. As if any of that helps. All the while we are surrounded by nothing but reminders of the support we have on this planet.

This is all well and good, you might say, but how to remember this, when you are at your lowest and most desperate?

How to connect with this when your mind is so exhausted that you cannot leave the house? How to connect with this if you are feeling lower than low and want to give up, or when you are so anxiety-ridden that you cannot make out your own hands, never mind a leaf or two?

For many reasons, many of us tend to sink as the day wears on. Some of us feel it in the morning, but for many years I was prone to feeling quite low in the late afternoons, when the morning optimism had long since drifted away. Often, by mid-morning I had quite simply run out of everything that I needed. I was moving from one nervous tic to another and strung out by evening. Living like this was not easy or sustainable.
I was fast losing the will.

What was I to do?

When your head is so full of pitch-gray, and everything feels meaningless and indistinct, you have to take it right back to the start.

What is the start?

When I am standing beside myself and cannot quiet my ever-running mind, the only thing I am inclined to do is to behave as a child might, when they are doing something that has their complete, rapt attention. The most soothing thing I can think of is to become completely immersed in a single action.

Why do I find this important?

It is a skill we lose as we grow. Out of necessity we find ourselves constantly problem-solving, multitasking, and thinking about the next thing. Usually what precedes a bout of exhaustion and depression is a mind that is running us out of town. Trying to slow down by becoming rapt about one thing is a breath of relief, is cool running water, is peace.

There is a pure, unmatched joy in what we call simplicity. Spending time outdoors, creating and preparing a meal, writing out lists. It is helpful to develop little projects: painting a picture or a room, creating something, whatever that might be. The activity is not paramount, it is the attention to the activity that matters. The interested, pure, and loving attention.

But why do I suggest this? How did I arrive here?

I cannot say why I am moved to this instinct, other than spirit (the energy and knowing that is locked away in all of us). Perhaps it was the sheer desperation of the downward spirals that brought forth clarity. Satisfaction is simple science, but it is not easy. There have been times in my life when I have underestimated the necessity of my own mindfulness. My mind was running amuck, but I did not know that it was controlling me, creating more discomfort. I was twitchy and unsettled and I did not know how to manage it. Every time I went to take a walk or eat in a restaurant with people, I would itch to come home. Lots of things about lots of things would bother me: the chewing gum stuck to the floor, the idea of germs, bad weather, noise, someone running behind me, people moving around too quickly or sneezing or suddenly laughing. I called it stress and it probably was. They called it OCD and it might have been. I did not call it a breakdown, but it was true that everything outside of my bed felt like the Wild Wild West. I thought it was the energy in all of the rooms in all of the places. I shut myself in the house and burned sage. I thought the vibrations of others might be too much for me. I called myself an empath. Perhaps. But while all of these things are valid, they are all still words . . .

and I had enough words to be dealing with.

One day, at the end of yet another overwhelming week, I took a day off.

I was on my way to brunch. Imagine.

I was on my way to brunch and the sun was shining.

I was on my way to brunch and the sun was shining, and I was holding hands with my lover. Imagine. A lover who loved me. Imagine. A lover who I loved, who loved me.

The thing was (and there is always a thing): there was something absent at my core. I had no sight left for the beauty. That afternoon, I was walking by four students who were painting a fence. The fence was metal, and the paint was thick, a deep bottle green. Something about it was deeply satisfying. I paused to view the hypnotic sight. I was mesmerized; the action looked positively luxurious. We were on our way to brunch, but I did not want to go. I wanted to throw myself on the ground and weep. All I could think about was how much I would like to be painting a bottle-green fence in the sun and not going anywhere and not holding hands with my lover. I wanted to do what they were doing. I wanted to be in my body.

It feels silly to think about it now. There I was, romanticizing the experience of other people, people who were doing a job that they might well have liked to leave to go off to brunch. They may not have thought the action luxurious. (It was certainly a projection.) I was privileged and ungrateful: I had so many things in this moment, but they were wasted on me. I had no sight for the beauty of my situation. I was too burned out. I could not appreciate anything in that moment other than the brushstrokes, the up-and-down motion,

the meditation of it,

the green, green fence. My mind was frazzled. Staring at that fence was a break from a body that was doing things on autopilot. A body that was doing things that I could no longer feel.

One thing at once, my inner being was saying: SIMPLIFY.
REST. One thing at a time. Slow it down. Paint the fence. Be
intentional and you will begin to be happy with what you
have. Try to do everything and you will be happy with
nothing.

Look for the moments this week in which you feel the most
and the least joyful or light. For the next seven days, divide
the day into four-hour intervals between waking and sleep-
ing. At each point of the day, write down the following: What
am I doing? Do I feel alive doing this? Do I feel a positive
response in my body? If not, what would I prefer to be doing
in this moment? Anything goes. These notes are only for you.

What patterns do you notice, looking at what you have writ-
ten down? What can you change, to avoid experiencing more
of the very same?

Tomorrow (as We Know It)
Is Never Promised

allowing and accepting

Sometimes life does interesting things. Sometimes they are angering and devastating, and in turn, we are forever altered. Sometimes they are lovely. Sometimes it's nothing we could have expected or predicted, and we struggle to find the tools to respond to the ever-changing landscape. It will always happen. That is how it goes. If there are quotidian things dear and important to us that we find ourselves taking for granted, let us really consider why we allow that to happen. In truth, we can never take it for granted that we will be here or that we are definitely meeting in our place next week, or that the show will go on, or that I get to hug you at the airport next month. Such is life, and that's alright. It is not our job to control things. Seasons will come, as will joy and excitement and terror. We will always be taken by surprise. That is the very nature of being a wild and moving part of a wild and moving universe. We maneuver, we innovate, we switch lanes in response, we learn, we adapt, we co-create. Tomorrow (as we know it) is never really promised. Wars, pandemics, and politics rip us from our seats. They show us things that we could never ever have anticipated. Although we have a powerful hand in creation, we cannot foresee every single event. Furthermore, why would we want to?

Think about something that recently uprooted you and threw you for a loop.

How would you have felt if you had known it was around the corner?

How would you have behaved differently preceding the event?

Who would you have spent more time with prior to the event? Who would you have spent less time with?

What might you have said or not said?

Perhaps current circumstances now mean that what you have written down is no longer possible. Of course, the past is over. Perhaps what you have written now is no longer possible. People, places, and things may have shifted out of your reach, but you can still use these findings to affect your movements and behavior, right where you are standing, right in this moment. Perhaps you make more time for something or someone you love. Perhaps you show up where you have been absent.

Perhaps you are kinder to yourself. Perhaps you decline when you want to.

Perhaps you say yes. Perhaps you tell the truth.

How to Maintain Equilibrium

*(when no one around you is
maintaining theirs)*

One of the most interesting aspects of humanness/humanity is that many of us are able to intuit, receive, and grow responsive to the energies of humans around us. Some of us, in fact, take special pride in recognizing the signals, cues, and needs of others—and congratulate ourselves on knowing exactly what to do to make someone else feel good. We are of an empathic nature, we say. We care so much about people, we say, or rather, we care so much what they think about us.

The greater issue is this: overidentification with the desires of others causes dissonance with our own personal journey.

Overinvesting in what other people think will eventually cause us to behave in ways that are not true to us. We will be so distracted trying to alter our presentation to suit the world that we will not hear our own inner guidance. Most of us do this at some time or another, quieting our insides to listen to someone else's. This is how we allow ourselves to be pulled into uncertain action, things we are not so sure about.

In truth, there is nothing kind or innocent about this. It is still fairly self-serving. Trying to have everyone fall in love with you is much the same thing as being invested in a result or condition in order to be happy. It is a type of manipulation. This lack of honesty is the same as not trusting.

If we were to become more deeply tuned in to our own hearts, we would behave in ways that are more genuine. We'd create deeper, more unconditional connections. We wouldn't be nearly as desperate for the validation or the results, because we would already be completely fulfilled in our own truthful existence. Thus, we would save so much time and confusion in our dealings. By remaining faithful to ourselves in this way, we would also strengthen our self-esteem.

We would save ourselves, too, from the inevitable resentment that meets us further down the line. When reviewing the things that we allowed within a relationship or friendship, it is common to become enraged at the things that took place, the grievances accrued. But how could we have known? We were not tuned in to ourselves. Of course, it pains us to think about some of the things that we let happen. With hindsight, we vow never to abandon ourselves again. Sound familiar?

It all comes down to trust and confidence in what we have, confidence that we are enough. Confidence enough to know that our worthiness does not depend on everyone agreeing with, identifying with, or even liking us.

Imagine a rare and exclusive conservatory bearing unique and wonderful produce. This one-of-a-kind ecosystem requires specific conditions in order to thrive. We cannot afford too extreme a change in the temperature, and we cannot allow certain dangerous materials or people in there either. If we want our fruit to flourish and be preserved at its very best, we must be selective. We cannot leave the door open at night or crank the heat up too high. We must be particular, and we must be precise.

Well, you are one of a kind. Thankfully, you are not a conservatory or a greenhouse, so I do not suggest that you should never be around unknown energies, or that everything in your life must be controlled beyond all reason. Some risks are good risks. Many people are good people, and so much life springs from the unknown. Trust yourself. Take your own temperature. Let your own being instruct your movement. Trust your source.

You are already growing more mindful in order to better understand the things that aid and harm you. We know that stress (cortisol), sleeplessness, disagreements, gossip, and comparison all bring about less than favorable conditions in the physical and emotional body. We must become gardeners and curators of our minds. We must pay attention to what we allow in, assessing what and who is able to freely gain access to us. Again, this is both practice and skill.

But it is easier to say it than to carry it out, and much of it comes back to the deep-rooted tendencies to people-please. Even today, I have friends or family members who tell me things about their lives, and if they are not having a great experience, it can sit with me for hours (or days) if I haven't done the necessary steps to look after myself first. If I feel unmoored to begin with and then I am given terrible news, something that sits in the base of my stomach, I find myself wishing that I never picked up the phone. I used to feel guilty about this. I used to feel like a bad friend. I now know that it is not about loving or not loving, but that I must ground myself, and on days when I don't feel grounded, I should take the necessary steps to protect my energy. In short, I cannot always be available. When I have clearly identified my own capacities, I am a more grounded and fair human being. I should not disrespect myself or my union with anyone else by overextending. Ignoring our own boundaries will surely result in resentment, exhaustion, and stress, and when we allow these boundaries to be crossed, we are absolutely responsible, and are less likely to be of any real or honest use or comfort to anyone else. Be open to the understanding that there are days and circumstances when your capacity may be more or less than usual. It works both ways. Please be a friend to yourself first, and never expect anyone to do a better job of it. No lover, no close friend, no family member. No matter how closely you hold each other, never give them the responsibility of looking after your heart.

It is a cop-out and a hostage situation. It is also impossible, since you are the only one who can make a life out of prioritizing and fulfilling your expectations. And haven't you yourself stumbled many times?

On the days when what we have built for ourselves is strong and unwavering enough, it will not matter who we are around and what their agenda or disposition is. Further to that, when what we have is strong enough, we will be less inclined to be in the company of those who are not a vibrational match. If work or circumstances call for exposure to them, they will not affect us, because we will be so finely tuned in to our home frequencies. We will know and understand how to maintain our own peace, even when it is openly challenged.

Identify what your new boundaries are in your key relationships. Discuss them with those whom you love, those with whom you can have a mature and honest exchange. Take turns identifying recent situations in which you did not make your boundaries clear enough and then, laying history aside, offer up new, better feeling alternatives.

The next time you experience a strong emotion in relation to an exchange you are having with someone, lay it out in front of you, identifying the parts that make it up.

Right away, why does it feel so tender?

Are emotional or physical boundaries being crossed, or have they been crossed in the past?

Who is involved? What does this relationship mean to you?

Does the relationship mean the same as it always has?

In this exchange, which of these feelings genuinely belong to you, and which to the other?

Do you feel a tendency to "fix," or offer up solutions?

Do you feel safe here, at your most honest?

What has been said or shown to you, or what do you fear might be said or shown to you? What is the root of the thing that you fear?

IN THE MORNING, FIND YOUR STATE FIRST. FIND THE PLEASING, PERSONAL FREQUENCY THAT YOU ARE HAPPY TO CALL HOME. NOTICE HOW YOU FEEL WHEN YOU ARE ALONE WITH IT. ASSOCIATE IT WITH SCENT. MUSIC. MOVEMENT. A PATTERN OF BREATH. USE SCENT TO GUIDE YOU HOME, USE MUSIC TO GUIDE YOU HOME, USE MOVEMENT TO GUIDE YOU HOME, USE BREATH TO GUIDE YOU HOME. KEEP WHAT BELONGS TO YOU AND NO ONE ELSE. HAVE A CLEAR IDEA OF HOW YOU WOULD LIKE TO FEEL FOR AS MANY PARTS OF THE DAY AS YOU CAN IMAGINE. DO NOT BE RESPONSIBLE FOR ANYONE'S HAPPINESS. YOU CANNOT CHANGE THEIR MOOD UNLESS THEY ARE A WILLING PARTICIPANT. FIND YOUR STATE FIRST. DECLINE AN INVITATION TO DISCORD OR CHAOS. IF YOU FEEL THAT THE ENERGY YOU ARE EXCHANGING WITH SOMEONE HAS SUDDENLY CHANGED, EXCUSE YOURSELF AND FIND YOUR STATE FIRST. HYDRATE. STRETCH. FEED YOURSELF. SPEAK TO PEOPLE MATCHING YOUR FREQUENCY. FIND YOUR STATE FIRST. NURTURE YOUR OWN UNIQUE AND BLISSFUL WORLDS AND FALL INTO THEM DAILY.

Body as Tremendous
Temporary Home

aka your wonderland

We can't have a conversation about The How and leave the body out of it. If we are not radical and fastidious about how we respect our physical bodies—everything from washing and gentle movement to the number of hours that we will allow ourselves to rest—then the body is usually the house to pay. We are not our bodies, but we are the keepers and gardeners of them, renting prime space inside for as long as we can manage it. Generally, we do not think enough of this privilege and commitment. We remember our bodies in pain or worry about the threat of pain. We remember them in illness or the idea of illness. We fear the fragility of our homes. Whenever pain has passed, if it has passed, we marvel at its strength. But mostly, we ignore the body in all of its constancy. As partners, we are hugely disloyal. Even when our bodies are praised, we complain about how they could be better still. We have berated our bodies and compared them and starved and poisoned them plenty. We have forced our bodies into desperate things and buried them under people, stress, diets, beauty standards, excess, substances, and work.

Why don't you take a walk inside?

Gently become aware of the sensation in your crown, whatever that sensation is.
Is it heavy or light?
Does it tingle or pulse? Is it tight?

This is the top constellation of your home. Acknowledge your dome, perforated with scores of points of energy and light. Be aware of the oxygen moving around it, cleansing and regenerating your cells.

Put your thought behind your forehead, in soft, circular movements. Hold it there.

Feel the patterns projecting images. Observe, and focus on the in and out of your breath.

Let your consciousness slip deep into the back wall of your mind, the rear wing, where all your new beauty is alive and forming. Let it sit and rest against the base of your skull.

Feel your pulse in the unique, familiar features of your face, your temples, cheekbones,
the deep rooms behind the eyes,
the bridge and tip of the nose,
the pulse where your tooth meets the gumline.

Pull your attention to the back of your throat and feel the passage of your breath. Breathe into the hollow of your neck. Relax those shoulders.

Draw your focus to your chest, where you hold all of the unsayable.
Soften your face and eyes.

Sense the whole scene around you, what is in front and behind. The more you relax and allow, the more you will feel. You are older here than you ever have been and younger than you will ever be

—oldest and youngest at the same time, how stunning a puzzle. In the present, you are always new.

It is no accident that you are here in this place, in this week, in this country, reading this, locating yourself time and time again in several parts of your body. Your beats, pulse, chemistry all exist for you and you alone, and they exist for a purpose. Look at the behind-the-scenes work it took to get you to this point. There's an organized crew underneath your skin. Happenings that are measured, essential.

Each time you feel as though everything that you can think of to say has been said before and that everything you can think of to do has been done already, remember that this is an untruth, for there is only one you that exists right here and in all of time, one you with your deliberate and delicate arrangement, one you that could never be replicated. In five years or even five months, you will wish that you had just started the thing (whatever your thing is) with or without worry. It is a hot thing to carry, knowing that you are not living out your purpose, knowing that you are the only one stopping yourself. It burns holes in all of your quiet corners. Be kind, and be kindest of all to yourself. You do what you do, and you do what you can, and those moving things are largely hidden and evolving. Over and over again, you get to choose. Every new minute, you get to choose. Your greatest ideas are already alive, turning themselves free in your body.

Think about what is new inside you today. Become aware of the life and existence in the forgotten parts of you. Everyone has forgotten parts to them.

Connect your mind to your body, breathing in the places where there is sensation, taking two or three minutes to become aware of yourself on a cellular level, of all the life and information, of the things that are possible today, physically, emotionally, or otherwise. Notice anything new that occurs to you.

Bring it softly into your awareness,
and then let everything loose. Let everything go.

BODY AS UNIT. BODY AS BASE CAMP. BODY AS AUXILIARY VEHICLE, AS EXCELLENT MODE OF TRANSPORT. BODY AS TREMENDOUS TEMPORARY HOME. BODY AS THE VERY PRESENT. BODY AS RECIPIENT OF SOURCE. BODY AS GIFT FROM ANY GOD YOU LIKE. BODY AS MAGNETIC ENERGY FIELD. BODY AS CELESTIAL PRIVILEGE. BODY AS OWN DAMN UNIVERSE. BODY AS TOP-LEAGUE SCHOOL OF HIGHER LEARNING. BODY AS STORYBOOK. COMIC. TELLTALE. LAST WORD.

Only Dreaming

(on that special time of the night)

When we dream, we tend to dream out of context. We dream large and surreal. We dream ridiculous. People change into other people, or perhaps we invent what we have never seen. We are not held back by the bounds of *what makes sense*. The heart is at work when the sun is down, and the night is a blue-black box that we inhabit—creative, cleansing, and complete. The dreaming part is important because our conscious minds are limited. Many times, our dreams contain the answers to the very questions we are asking. When we are dreaming, we are further out of the way of our own wishes. We are all creators. You are a sorcerer and so am I.

When you wake up in the morning, use what you have before it slips away. Keep a notebook by your bed and write it down.

Catch the thought. See who and what is communicating with you, which formulas are opening up to you.

For an even more potent sample:

Set an alarm to wake yourself up at a strange time of the morning, some three hours before you usually rise, and when you wake, free write as much as you can. This is a special time for the shaping of things, the black notes of the dream self. Throw down thoughts, not neatly or elegantly but just because you are here and you can and the thoughts are dripping through you like rain, as though you were a clear vessel for inspiration. Go back to sleep. Rest well.

When Awakening

on shaping the day

In any given morning, when you wake, you have a small and distinct opportunity to set your mind and intention. You have a good few seconds where the order of things is undecided—when the wolflike thing has not yet arrived at your door; when the bills, or aches, or woes have not yet sung out to you; when your trauma is a sleeping animal, when you're not yet thinking about what somebody said or is going to say to you today at work. You have a clean and clear window to set your brain in the preferred direction. Use the first twenty seconds or so to make intentions, to practically intend, to decide what today will be to you. Attention and resonance must be weighed in how you want to feel, rather than goals and outside events. You are a great reflector, which is why days can have this mystical potential; it is all a question of what we see and what we don't see, what we allow ourselves and what we won't. Yes, every last thing in life, no matter how grand or subtle, is a question of perception, but perception can be curated. The art of perception is a skill, like any other. Develop it today and make up your own music. What is a day but a series of beats punctuated by light?

Wake, and while the sleep is still in your eyes, consider the possible and preferred feelings of several parts of the day. Plan as wide and wild as you like—who is there to curb you? Soft-focus on how each part will feel. Then, when you are clear enough, begin your day.

Consider your findings once you have spent a week or so working on morning intentionality. What has changed?

Find Me in the Morning

before the day has done its work on us.

While I'm un-punched, limber, in line with the stars.

Potassium. Closer to the bed of the universe. Find me

traveled, while I can still hear my mother's voice,

while my fear is upside down and I am petal,

I am unfettered, silver-soft, and I hear singing.

Find me at the top of the light while I am exchanging with my

ancestors; far from the terror of everything. Find me open-

souled, dense with hope. Find me.

Mind Violence

the time warp; the pretty trap

Of course, we must touch upon The Phone. The metal-and-glass rectangle taking up all time and space; containing whole wide worlds. This time-devouring portal, both toxic and absolute, this machine transcending continents and time zones. This sci-fi we are always consumed with, even when we are trying to inspire something real, even when we are attempting to be one-on-one. It disrupts our peace and our brain waves and sleep, swallowing many of our new and budding ideas. I love my phone and I hate my phone. The Phone facilitates connection and laughter, sex, attraction, and wonder. The Phone is a wealth of opportunity. And The Phone is a seductive, incessant tomb. We can only be the sum of our focus. Let's be clear and largely awake in our choosing.

Every single day requires a phone-free period. Even if you can only manage less than an hour. Even if you have a job that requires use of your phone. Even if you have dependents. Take that time away from the phone and see what relief it brings. If you have become so attached (as we all do), you may experience edginess and separation anxiety upon doing this. All the more reason to slowly dismantle it. None of us who takes part in social media is exempt from the growing addiction. After all, it is designed specifically for that purpose.

Turn off all unnecessary notifications that disrupt your day and weaken your attention span. Your phone may well be a large part of the reason you find concentrating on books or films difficult these days. Watching one-minute videos every day primes the brain toward short bursts of dopamine and curated information over anything that requires deeper work and concentration and elevated creativity.

Find another action every time you feel an uncontrollable urge to scroll or check messages. Use something else that fulfills you. Dynamic movement. Reading aloud. Writing down your thoughts.

If you live somewhere with more than one room, allocate one room where your phone is not allowed. If nowhere else, it could even be the bathroom. If you can, keep it out of your bedroom area. Preserve your sacred haven.

Even the Greatest Love Is Work

love, the inside job

They tell us to love ourselves. They tell us to love and care deeply for ourselves, and they say it is the solve-all. The great answer. But how to get there?

They tell us to check in with our friends, to really hear and support them when they are weary and disheartened. How to achieve that when we are not even checked in with ourselves? All love is one love. And even the greatest love is work.

In present culture, the ideas of self-love and deep care of the self are so co-opted and monetized that they have been made to appear somewhat trite. If you find yourself struggling with the very notion of loving yourself, or if it sounds clichéd and unrealistic, let us explore the concept further. Self-love is not bath salts, a trip away, chocolate, or a wellness product—it does not have a two-hundred-dollar price tag. Self-care is not veganism or shopping or homeware. It is not cosmetics or exercise. Everything helps, but it is the intention and inspired action, not the product. Simply put, self-love and self-care are deep commitments to the things that nourish you and the termination of what does not. It is listening, being present with yourself, allowing the things that you have outlined and identified—the things that you love and need.

And what of romantic love? How many times have we thought about love as an end point, the answer to our woes? How often have we thought of love as a great destination? It is absolutely true that real love has transformational power. But this is a power you ignite in yourself. You see a reflection in the object of your affection, but it is always, always you. In every case, you make your own good magic. You can only ever feel with the contents of your own soul. You can only love as much as you *know* love.

Romantic love will never work as a solve-all, and it will never work in the way that most of us have hoped. It will not take you from beast to beauty, from desperate hopelessness to sudden enlightenment. Many of us see the romantic other as someone who will make us feel better in our skin, someone who will surely give us purpose. But you get the lover, maybe even the one of your dreams, and then they refuse to be the answer; they refuse to provide you a reason to live. How dare they?

One year I was so "in love" that I forgot to eat. Can you believe it? I took away my food and I called it *love*. A friend who was watching me grew worried. He saw the pits under my eyes and likened my weekends away with my lover to a weekend of doing drugs. He wasn't wrong. There was something unchecked and desperate in the way that I was using what I called *love*: the high of being chosen against the growing fear and danger of the lover finding someone new. You see, I was in love with someone as troubled as I. There was an emptiness in the lover that I saw and called *mysterious*, a darkness that I wanted to fall into. I called the constant uncertainty *interesting*. I had not yet recognized the darkness as my own. (How unfair we are to those we obsess over, those we place high above us. Again and again, we dehumanize them.) Of course, it was all an illusion. The one I thought I loved turned out to be a mirror. How clumsy I was, overreaching, grasping for myself each time and coming away empty-handed.

No one can fix you. No one can complete you. We set others up to fail when we base our love on the fulfilment of expectations. Love for self is a completely inside affair, and as for loving another? This love is a vast, developing project to be nurtured with care and time. We are forever being shown examples in TV and films of when romantic love bursts into being, or disappears. Less spoken about is the moment when love becomes something that you show up for, a decision you make. Work. Diligent, caring work. Sometimes it feels more about commitment than passion. But isn't commitment a kind of passion? Actually, you make the rules. You can make a passion of anything. Once we reach this understanding, we will have uncovered one of the great secrets of the work of love.

Perhaps we search for the same thing in different iterations. Growing up with my grandparents, I would miss my mother so much that I would pretend to dislike her. It was easy. She was always away. As I got older, I began to understand and treasure her, viewing her as a full and complex human being. Imagine! Just like myself! Slowly, I began to understand what motivated some of her more enigmatic behaviors. While it was not my job to judge or even to excuse, a little understanding helped. It brought us a little closer. She was a human, with her own agenda and desires. I would never meet the mother I dreamed of, the mother I idealized. That person does not exist. I considered, then, all of the things that I was so desperately searching for that I could probably provide for myself.

Think for a moment about the attributes that you searched for in a lover that might have sprung from an early feeling of lack. What were you in search of? Was it acceptance? Confidence? Reassurance? How did it feel when you were at last able to fulfill some of those needs yourself? If you haven't quite gotten there yet, think of some things you look for in your dream partner.

Growing up, what was the first thing that confused you about the way your caregivers loved? And now, in love, what is the thing you are always trying to obtain? Why, if you feel it lacking in the very core of yourself, do you think someone else can give it to you? And how do you think you would be best placed to give it to anyone else?

Keep a treasured notebook in which you write down all of your positive attributes.

Add to it every single week as you discover more and more.

When you learn something wonderful about yourself and wonder what else you've been hiding,
you learn that
1. you are not done
   (and)
2. you are never done.

I WILL LOVE ME, DESPITE ANYTHING. WHEN I AM BEING TALKED ABOUT, WHEN I AM UNNOTICEABLE, WHEN MY BEAUTY IS DEBATED, WHEN MY WORTHINESS IS CALLED INTO QUESTION. EVEN WHEN I AM THE BAD THING, AS I AM SURE SOMETIMES TO BE. EVEN AS I BURN WITH SHAME. I WILL RISE UP FROM MY HIDING PLACE AND LOVE MYSELF CLEAN AND THROUGH. THIS LOVE, A DAILY PROFESSION. THIS LOVE, A GENUINE LIFELINE.

The Desire Behind the Desire

our hidden motivations, and the

truth behind them

What do we need? What do we want? Many of our true motivations have become a mystery to us. I may claim that I want to do well in my career and make good money, though if I travel some way back, I will see that this desire stems from a great need to be recognized and seen, because I have in the past felt invisible, which stems from an even earlier primal need for love and connection. I still remember the root and its origin. But sometimes our causes have long disappeared from us. All that is left is the neon sign: the need.

Whatever old or new thing we are doing, we do in the hope that it will make us feel better. The problem arises when we repeat actions again and again, not because they breed anywhere near satisfactory results, but rather because we have trained ourselves to do so. In every single moment we are teaching ourselves how to be and respond. The brain does what it does so easily because of a series of repetitions. This is why habits develop as quickly as they do. You do or think something a few times, and before you know it, a pattern has emerged. You've created a neural pathway. But if we are basing our actions on an old want, an old feeling of unworthiness, one that has no standing in where our lives are this very day, we will continue to behave in ways that don't serve us.

We can unpick the old knots. Every habit can be unlearned. We owe it to ourselves to discover the desire behind the desire, so we can make choices based on what is really best for us. Once we discover the core reasons for our behavior, we will be better placed in understanding what we think we are missing. We owe it to ourselves to notice patterns in our thinking and behavior that might be leading to the same old unsatisfactory results. We owe it to ourselves so we may better understand our behavior and infuse it with more clear-sightedness, more truth.

For years I wanted to write and act and make creative work that would appeal to the masses. There were so many conflicting desires behind my desire. I wanted people to like me and be impressed by me. I wanted to stand out and I wanted to fit in and be accepted. This was a contradiction, and it is why my truth failed.

I wrote my first novel when I was seventeen, and the book was about four middle-class white British women who were nothing like me. Still, I wondered why the work didn't *work*. The problem was not chiefly that I was trying to write characters who were not Black. The problem was the dissonance—that, because of the culture I was in and around, the very idea of writing characters who were Black and trying to sell that commercially did not even occur to me. Unconsciously, I was trying to build what I thought would be successful instead of what my heart was urging me to write. I had not even conceived that there could be a market for the genre-shifting stuff that was going on in my head. I had not conceived that there was a market for weird Black characters doing nuanced, extraordinary things. I was not exposed to such and I had lost imagination. All I needed to do, though, was to write about what excited me. To write about myself. To use my imagination. If I felt it, the publisher might have felt it too.

We have to be true to our own inner guide. We have to trust our work. If we are artists, truth is the only way in which we can make the work truly resonant and urgent. If we are true about what we are feeling, no matter how specific, it will become universal.

That is why, when your work meets the air, there is nothing to fear. When you are expressing yourself with everything that you have and creating art about your various truths, there is nothing to lose, because your feelings are our feelings. A lot of us are experiencing somethings, and those somethings mean they can relate to you.

Think about the paintings, poems, books, and songs that you love the most. Think about why it is that you love them. Is it because they're pretty, and show the artist or subject in a favorable way? Rarely. You love them because they are a bridge all the way into the soul. You love them because they shine a light somewhere inside. Oftentimes the artist is rendered invisible, and it is the feeling that remains. We enjoy and we relate to and understand and love the desperate and heavily flawed characters we see on television and in books, even in their most despicable actions, because they reflect and appeal to a part of us. They get away with saying or doing things that a lot of us secretly think about. They steal, lie, make mistakes; they do the forbidden, the perverse, the unthinkable. They manipulate. These characters tell the truth even when they lie—because *we* can see their truth, and we recognize ourselves.

When you are honest in whatever you are becoming or creating, never worry about giving away too much of yourself. Since your truths are forever shifting, the more you give away, the more you keep.

What are the main themes running through your life? What things come up again and again? What feelings are you most at home with?

When we can see what our running themes are, we can begin to build up a picture. The reason the picture is not clear right away? Well, we are in the middle of it. We are far too deep inside the mix, our eyes are turned outward.

Take the next two days to note specific themes, where they ring in the body and what they mean to you. Do not try to interpret or assess; just observe the feeling as a shifting fact, a story element.

If your life were a film, which genre would it be? A comedy, a family drama, a thriller, or a farce? In other words, what themes go on and on appearing? What are you ready to end? And what are you ready to start?

Beginning

starting: a science

The trick to starting a thing is knowing that no one else has been called to this the same way as you. It doesn't matter if it seems as though everyone else is doing the same thing. Do not be disheartened by this lie. Your trajectory cannot be compared to that of anyone else.

The trick to starting a thing is remembering that it can be easy to be confused about what to do first, and that confusion can easily become inertia. It can be so easy to sit there, not knowing the way in. I pushed so many projects to the side because I believed that I didn't know the right way in, and so allowed myself to be put off, right at the start. Most things that we haven't learned yet appear more difficult than they really are, whether financial, spiritual, or technical. Some things are set up that way to retain the illusion of exclusivity, so that they may deter the outsider.

Everything in the entire world can be broken down, if you take the steps carved into the mountain and forget the size of the mountain itself. Everybody who ever did anything started with the smallest movements. So now, what are yours?

The trick to starting a thing is surrounding yourself with the things in life that inspire you. Anything that creates movement in the well of your being, be it art, literature, visuals, or people. The emphasis here is not on analysis. Sure, there are people paid to critique and review, but think about how art, performance, and music affect *you*. We do not always know why something moves us, but simply that it does, and that is enough. Dedicate times in each day when you allow yourself to become immersed in something that stirs you. If you make time for this each day, you will, in time, be influenced to begin.

The trick to starting a thing is allowing yourself to be carried by the initial momentum that made you want to do it. Begin today, because you will not feel the same way tomorrow.

This weekend, begin something new that has a lot of steps to it. Something that seems almost off-putting in its length. Begin by taking the first step of many. Make this first step as enjoyable as you can—draw it out. Savor it.

Ending

finishing: a science

The trick to finishing a thing is understanding the currency of focus. We must protect our brains, our exquisite tuning forks. You already know that you can do it, and you don't need anyone to tell you. Your opportunities or lack of them led you to this unique and blessed point.

The trick to finishing a thing is starting the thing every day, at around the same time, with some kind of will. Even if nothing good seems to be emerging. Even if the only moving things are on the other side of the window. The trick to finishing a thing is showing up for it, even just to stare. Even just to make moves that feel inconsequential, even just to delete everything you did yesterday, even just to sigh. Show up and you remind yourself that what you care about is worth it, that you are worthy. It is about more than the activity. It is about being there for yourself.

The trick to finishing a thing is breathing into it. Giving it a name and a color and some kind of identity, some voice. Letting it exist in its own space in this universe, letting it be born. A slow birth, though it feels like torture, is the best kind of birth there is: a low, glacial forming. Breathe into the thing. Treat it as a tiny, delicate being on its holy journey, and even when you cannot see it growing, look at it with as much love as you can muster.

Everything has the potential to shock you with its progress, to bloom, to change state. In the end, time does not matter. In the end everything becomes something else. There is no stage of being that is more important than any other. Even if you feel as though you might never finish a thing, never let it prevent you from starting. Be in love with the idea of it and admire it every day. Allow yourself to think about it with only admiration and imagination.

List five things that you have not completed that you feel uneasy about. Choose two of these five things to begin again. Take the time to complete them. Look at them and try to imbue yourself with all the passion that you initially had when you started. Approach each task at a time, and then begin. You deserve many beginnings.

Truthwork

the beauty of shifting detail

In any one moment, there are a thousand truths. Ever hear the phrase "As you see it, so it is"? If so, depending on how we think about things, aren't there so many realms of possibility in any one scenario?

Here is an example.

Listen to the sound your parent/lover/child is making when you are engaged in an argument or difficult conversation.

Listen to the words, yes . . . but also for the sound, colors, dimension. Is there sun high above you? Is there rain? Do they love you, despite it all? Do you do everything in your power to love them the way you think you should? And so what is the truth today—the real truth?

Well, the answer is this: There are a thousand truths. There are always a thousand of them. Details like

- the wetness of the atmosphere when you changed your mind / lost a friend / finally said *no*

- the shocking orange-pink on the horizon at sunset, how it darkened before your eyes in minutes

- the powder white of the snow on the way into town when you were falling in love

- how quietly the trees were moving after an accident

- how when you last heard the words "we need to talk" you were already growing defensive; the night was silver and new, and you could hear the next-door neighbor singing show tunes through the wall

When all of the so-called "bad" things in life are happening to you and me and everyone else, there are still all of these gorgeous particulars, all of the things around that still love us. They remind us by still happening every day despite everything else. Water still ripples, the clouds are high above us, greenery is still pumping out oxygen, and we are sitting or standing in our bodies, aren't we? We are making use of this air, are we not? We can choose to think about the thousand different truths instead of the few more difficult ones. We can decide right now what to keep, what to rise from.

All this is easier said than done, right?
You can't ignore the facts, after all.
Perhaps not, if you say so. But you can start by seeing them, multiplying them, having options.

Treat the following as a journaling exercise, a writing or conversation prompt, or a meditation.

Think of a conversation or interaction you had recently with a loved one that changed your mood significantly. What was special about your surroundings? Color? Light? Temperature?

What did you notice right away about the person you were talking to?

Now acknowledge a fact about them. When they said what they said, did the air change?

What were you left with at the end? And thinking about it again today, what more do you know?

Why We Write It Down

working it out on the page

Writing is not only for the writers. When we write things down, we permit a range of cognition and memory that we do not employ by simply noticing or talking about something. When we write, we bring something cleanly into the present, with new eyes, today's eyes. The page is a place for magic to occur. Here we can turn things into precisely what we want. We can give fleeting and escaping things our full attention. We can allow them to bloom, to have their say. We talked about dreamwork and the art of letting things flow through. Free-writing (writing in a continuous flow about anything, everything, nothing) is a strong and powerful device to access the stuff of dreams, for letting everything flow out.

I had an acting teacher who would tell us that when thinking about a character we were building, we should outline that character's specific need, using a real person and a mirroring scenario from our own life. For example, if the character was hopelessly in love, we would start with the prompt *I need you to love me because* . . . and just begin writing, about someone we felt that way about in real life. Often, we were surprised at the outcome—at what would appear in front of us. *That's really how I feel?*

We found that we still harbored anger about things that had taken place a long time ago, and we found that there were some questions for which we were still desperately seeking answers. In any case, there is a whole iceberg-size thing that we push deep into our subconscious, made up of details that we haven't engaged with in years, or ever. Writing helps us locate and release. If you are afraid to say the thing, write the thing.

Write down, in a stream of consciousness, without pausing, something you did not say today but wish you had. It doesn't even need to make sense; don't judge it. Just write.

Write down a message to a loved one, a message that you are unlikely to send, telling them something that they do not know about you.

Write down an account of an interaction you had today in which you did not reveal how you really felt. Stop at nothing. Write as though no one else you know will ever see this. After writing, choose whether to keep or discard the page.

These exercises are more for a loosening, a shaking of the rug. The freedom is more important than the content. What we hold in our bodies can be used in myriad ways. Expression is relief, and surefire medicine.

YOU WRITE WHEN YOU NEED TO. YOU WRITE IT DOWN BECAUSE EVERYTHING HAS THE DAZZLING AND SURPRISING POTENTIAL TO TEACH, HEAL, BECOME WORK, BECOME ART. BECAUSE WHAT MEETS YOU ON THE PAGE WILL ALMOST CERTAINLY SURPRISE YOU. BECAUSE YOU WILL FIND NEW WAYS. THERE ARE ALWAYS NEW WAYS. BECAUSE IN WRITING WE CAN IMAGINE, TRANSFORM, INVENT INCREDIBLE AND NEVER-ENDING ALTERNATIVES, DREAM THINGS UP. BECAUSE HERE YOU ENSURE THAT NOTHING WILL EVER REALLY BE LOST. AND IF THE WORDS FALL, THEY WILL REACH OUT INTO BETTER PLACES, AND WHEN THE WORDS FALL, THEY WILL DIVIDE AND LAND ON SOMEONE WHO NEEDS THEM MORE THAN EVEN YOU. BECAUSE HERE YOU ALLOW ALL YOUR EXPERIENCES TO BECOME USEFUL. BECAUSE WRITING AND SOLVING AND CREATING = ALCHEMY. BECAUSE YOU CAN NEUTRALIZE OLD, OLD THINGS THAT STILL BURN. BECAUSE WHEN YOU MAKE ART YOU PLACE YOURSELF IN A BLESSED STATE OF POWER, POWER TO CREATE, POWER TO CHANGE THE WORLD BY CHANGING HEARTS, POWER TO REACH OUT, POWER TO SUBVERT, POWER

TO TELL THE TRUTH FOR ONCE, POWER TO BIRTH A NEW TRUTH, POWER TO BE IN LOVE WITH AN UNTAMED AND MOVING THING. POWER NOT TO BE WEIGHED DOWN BY WHAT HAS BEEN, WHAT ALMOST WAS, AND WHAT MIGHT NEVER BE. BECAUSE WHEN YOU WRITE YOU AWAKEN THE DEEP, ALL-KNOWING POWER, THE CREATOR, THE EVER-PRESENT NARRATOR. POWER TO CHANGE SHAPE, POWER TO DRAW OUT WHAT YOU DIDN'T KNOW WAS IN THE WAY. POWER TO BECOME. POWER TO KEEP ON BECOMING AND NEVER, EVER STOP. POETRY. POWER TO SPARK, LIGHT UP, SET ON UNYIELDING AND EXCELLENT FIRE. POWER TO PUT IT OUT. POWER TO LET IT OUT AND LET GO. YOU MAKE IT BECAUSE IF YOU DON'T, WHO ELSE WILL? YOU WRITE IT BECAUSE IF YOU DON'T, WHERE DOES IT GO? WHAT BECOMES OF HIDDEN, MUTATING THINGS THAT ARE NOT ALLOWED TO HAVE THEIR DAY? WHAT BECOMES OF THE BRILLIANT THINGS LEFT ALONE AND UNFED? YOU WRITE IT DOWN, BECAUSE WHY NOT? WHY NOT NOW? IF NOT NOW, THEN WHEN? YOU WRITE IT. YOU HAVE TO. PERHAPS ONLY YOU KNOW WHY.

The Three Percent

That awful three percent in you

thinks sadness is romantic.

Is aroused by unsavory things.

Wants the very worst thing to happen.

Wants everyone to want you

But doesn't know how to be loved.

Needs want. Wants, needs. Makes up stories

and sticks with them.

Can't be happy for your friends.

That horrible three percent in you thinks you'll be left behind.

Fears new things, old things, intimacy, loneliness,

children, childlessness, conflict, boredom,

isolation, silence, news.

That terrible three percent of you

is the reason it might fall through.

What does *your* three percent look like?

You Are Not the Only One.

Let that sit with you awhile. Everyone has a secret that tries
to tank them. Everyone has a truth that haunts the throat at
night. And we all wonder, is it normal?
Would they love me if they knew?
What would the moon and the stars say?
Nothing. They'll never talk.

Blessed Expertise

focus and personal choice

Do you ever consider the thousands of things you have learned, against the thousands of possibilities of other things that you *could* have learned? I might have learned instead about geodes and rock formations, countries of the world, stocks and business. The aforementioned are not the most important things in the world. But they might have been more useful than the things that I chose to fixate upon. In the past I became an expert on calorie counting, keeping up appearances, what not to say, how not to reveal myself, how to play my cards extremely close, how to inspire certain feelings in others in several self-seeking ways. We must not be too hard on ourselves. Often, we learned what we learned out of desperation, or some fearful attempt to protect ourselves.

When I was younger, I thought that being "nice" and "attractive" was one of the easiest ways to endear people to me. I minced my words and would agree with everyone I spoke to. I would litter sentences with qualifiers, and my true sense of self was entirely lost to me. Everyone at school thought I was their "best friend." Meanwhile, I was indifferent to them, because I could not be myself. This caused problems in several aspects of my life: sex and dating, work, money. I was always doing things I didn't really want to do. What's more, I could not stop.

You surely become an expert on the thing that you focus on, be it misery or mathematics. Have you ever watched someone who is set on dieting disappear with force in front of you? Ever watched a person make money in six different languages? Ever seen a lover charm everyone in the room—even in an entirely obnoxious moment? Models, off duty, still know how to make the camera find them, even if they do not want to be seen that day. It is a question of expectation and practice. The truth is this: Life happens in the places where we rest our attention, in the actions that we repeat. Those of us who are always laughing have a feeling of mirth about us. Those who always land on their feet are always finding new ways to succeed. Experiences that we are repeating are continually being written deeper and deeper inside us, always being added to the precious code that makes us up. We expect what we have experienced, and we come to experience what we expect.

In this way we can become fluent in anything we practice. We know this to be true because when we focus our attention on a thing like gratitude, we are able to rewire, to see the beauty in something before we go to complain. Even when we are dissatisfied, we are apt to see a silver lining on the situation.

Let us become active in the crafting of our own experience.

1. Think of something that you would love to happen,

   and begin to

2. Slow-nurture the expertise needed to bring it about.

And Are You Lonely?

how to be alone and joyful

Lonely is a mix of several unspecified, blue things. A response to a situation, the feeling of the absence of something. A stress response, a perception, a possible untruth. It can be an emotional and spiritual shortfall, an invitation to create more feelings of unworthiness. It can be discomfort, where we compare, where we believe we are less than, as though we might be missing something that everyone else has.

What is this feeling, exactly? From what place does it arrive? Is it real or largely imagined, and what difference does that make? If you are feeling it, isn't it "true" enough?
Most of us know this intense pang of nothingness, this endless dark mass and space for miles, this feeling of missing something vital to your insides—whether with a loved one or not.

Whether with a loved one or not.

This is an imbalance that begins at home, deep within. Loneliness happens at the party and after you have left

or it happens in bed with someone

or it catches up with you at family dinner

or at work

or when you are spending a lunchtime alone, unwrapping and chewing on fear.

It arises, anytime, anywhere. This is how you come to know that your solution can never be someone else. If you are lonely on your own, there is an excellent chance that you will be lonely with someone. Lonely with everyone. Because no one will save you from this feeling. No soul but your own has that power.

The times in my life when I felt loneliest correlate with times when I was not giving of myself, not talking to people, empathizing less, not making connections. Odd, then, that I still found myself surprised at being lonely, since I had a good idea how I caused it. But we are always failing to see ourselves. In the past, I adopted a kind of "lone" identity—which, I'll be honest, many parts of me really enjoyed—to keep the world away, and to free myself of any responsibility to my fellow humans. In doing so, I kept myself free of one kind of pain in exchange for another. But this was a false safety. During those times, I felt continually disappointed about things, all the while giving nothing myself.

Core loneliness is disconnection from ourselves and from the world around us. We forget that people (or the lack of people) or love (or the lack of love) is only ever a reflection. What you think is keeping you safe might be cutting off your air supply.

You do not have to feel like this. You have wandered a little way from yourself. Finding your way back begins with clarity: knowing what you *want*, instead of what you think you are missing. *Wanting* is not the same as pining for, fretting about, longing for. Wanting can be the most thrilling exercise—where fantasy and creation come into play. It begins, too, with desire. The most hopeful place on earth.

There is an inner change that must take place before you can perceive yourself and your surroundings differently. It is not the situation that will change you. It is you who will change the situation. If what you want is community, love, and understanding, you must become an example of a loving, understanding person who belongs (or is in the process of belonging) to a community. This is how you know such things exist, and how you attract more of the same.

If what you want is not to be lonely, then lonely cannot be an identity you build for yourself. It cannot be how you think of yourself. And, you are never truly alone—this is universally impossible. There is a multiverse that makes you up, and you are always walking in some abundance. You are surrounded, by thought, energy, sound, light, small miracles that you have stopped noticing or have yet to discover. You are made up of the things that you learn, the million parts of yourself, the landscapes, the growing nature you contain, your waters, your love. Focus on these things, take your attention to the things around and inside you—and the things that are yet to form. This is alchemy in action. This is how you get what you want.

Do not let dissatisfaction and impatience prevent you from enjoying the road to what you want. Do not waste your own time by focusing on the lack of the thing. Allow yourself the satisfaction of knowing that it is on its way. When what you want is an idea, your job is to find a way to believe it. Remember: Believe in what you want so much that you do not feel the lack, and trust in the arrival of the thing, as if you have ordered food or someone you love is on their way over to visit. Trust that the thing is on its way. Fantasy has immensely healing properties. Being content and excited right now does not mean you are happy to accept less; it is the very opposite. Everything from food to sex to holidays is more exciting when we are anticipating the joy of them, and when you see something incredible coming, you are actually already tapping into the feeling of the thing, the energy and the texture of it. That is why fantasy feels so good. From the moment the desire is sparked, you are already receiving, being fulfilled.

There are two ways to think about it; you can be alone and excited about what's to come or you can be alone and lonely. One of these ways of thinking is an opportunity for newness and delight, and one of them only ensures more of the same loneliness. I invite you to create with joy and passion . . . and have a good idea of what and whom you want around you. I invite you to go on attracting like things. You're full of them. Draw it, paint it, see it in your head before you go to sleep and get out of bed in the morning. Get the house ready. Believe in everything. Help it find you.

Describe the very experience of loneliness. How it feels. When and where you feel it, and what happens.

Describe the exact opposite to the feeling you just described, aiming to feel the thrill in your body, along with fantasy and with much description.

When you are at your loneliest, who and what are the common denominators?

What can you do today to help someone else who is facing feelings of loneliness?

What is something you can do right now, to remind yourself of your connection to the world? Is there a message you wanted to send, a compliment you wanted to give, a donation you wanted to make, a letter you wanted to write? Do it now.

TAKE AN EARLY MORNING OUTING, LISTEN TO THE EARTH HUM ITS TALE, GET ALL CAUGHT UP IN ONE TASK AT A TIME (WHETHER IT IS READING, SWEEPING THE FLOOR, OR BAKING A CAKE). FIND WIND-DOWN TIME A COUPLE OF HOURS BEFORE BED, DISCUSS YOUR MOST INTIMATE MORNING THOUGHTS WITH ANOTHER, LISTEN TO THE INTIMATE MORNING THOUGHTS OF ANOTHER, CUT YOUR MEDIA CONSUMPTION BY HALF, PRIORITIZE SOMETHING THAT FEELS GOOD EVERY SINGLE DAY, VISUALIZE SOMETHING YOU ARE LOOKING FORWARD TO (IN GREAT DETAIL). LET NEGATIVE EMOTIONS PASS OVER YOU, GENTLY, LIKE DREAMS.

Not the End of the Day

the question of grief

There is a special kind of loss that shocks the entire system. It happens when someone close is here one day and gone the next, after which all who remain are expected to carry on.

I am talking about death, which we can never fully be prepared for, whether it is unexpected or expected, whether it's of natural causes or following ill health, an extended battle that has stretched out across months. How to ever be truly prepared for the heartbreak, the shock of the thing? And then for the aftermath?

You wake up and for a moment you have forgotten that it is true. You wake up . . . and remember them gone. You still have their voice recording from last week and the photos you've been sharing all year. All of their clothes still hang in the wardrobe. You are wearing their coat. You cannot process this alarming new thing as truth. You stand in the weeds, disoriented. You wonder if it might be some terrible dream.

We don't talk about death. I don't know why we don't talk about death, since we are all brilliant, breathing time bombs, timeless and intuitively terminal. In school we are taught mathematics and theorems, literature and language. We are briefed in detail on the mechanics and function of sex and sexuality, though never the quiet certainty of death. We are taught about atoms and evolution, physics and the magic of biology, but never about the ending of a life force. We have neither details nor evidence. Nobody ever came back from the dead to tell us about it (or if they did, we did not believe them).

Yes, death is one of the largest mysteries of all. Is this why it is so taboo in our society—so untouched, so *hushed*? Nobody tells you the truth about losing one of your loves up close . . . and what might happen to your insides on hearing the news. Nobody warns you about the odd business of it all, that you have to do ordinary, upsetting, practical things: choosing a wood finish for a box for your beloved's body; calling the medical examiner to pronounce your loved one "dead"; choosing flowers or an appropriate plot or arguing over funeral catering; giving away their favorite clothes. The paperwork. The will. The house. All of this ordinary, dreadful work.

And the unprecedented grief of it, the slow thick grief of it—the full realization that sets in when the buffer of shock and business has finally gone away, when well-wishers have stopped calling you to ask how you are and have resumed their own lives. You are left alone with the reality: the person you love has transitioned and the world has shifted irrevocably, and somehow, everything around you is still allowed to go on. And no one, no one at all, tells you about the hidden black ice of it all: the anger at life itself, at the person you loved who is never to return. The grim, ugly jealousy that rises when you see friends who still have their lover/friend/family member. Those feelings that you have admitted to no one.

But here is a true thing about death: the only death that you will not survive is your own. There is no pain in the world that cannot move, that will not change shape. There is no pain in the world that will not shift into something more bearable. It is a little like adding a deep, pigmented color into a pot of white paint: it will not be forgotten, nor will it stay the same. The body will alter somewhat. You will be changed, perhaps forever. This is not a bad thing, for we are ever richer for having loved and lost—even if the initial loss has you on your knees. Blood-red and white equal pink. Hold the deepest blue to the light and you have sky, sky, sky for miles. You stare death in the face, and you are softer for having come up against the thing. All this, if you have the capacity to be open. In the end, you will feel it happen. You will become more vulnerable, more aware, and you will strengthen. There is no work or science to it. There is only the passing of time.

Sometimes, all there is to do is breathe. When the numbness has subsided (and it will), you will recognize new things in the eyes of your fellow humans everywhere. Love and our ideas of loss are the very elements that bind us. The vast processes of both help us to feel something for others. They help us realize that life surrounds us, and they can nudge us to remember to make joyful use of it.

Here's another thing (a thing we *did* learn at school): energy can neither be created nor destroyed. That is to say, whoever has gone is never, ever gone; they are simply nonphysical (after all, the physical is just one of the many manifestations of existence). Your loved one remains alive in all they have touched and created. Alive in you, and in the memories that revive them. Imbue yourself with the qualities of your beloved, all the things you admired. Adopt them as your own. Integrate something useful, something positive or affirming that you haven't had access to before. From their nonphysical form, allow them to inspire you, for nothing we have loved, have treasured, have held dear, is ever truly lost from us. Make new, deliberate, and inspired choices. Perhaps it was their generosity that you appreciated, a softness of the spirit. Perhaps it was a directness in tone, unflinching bravery. Perhaps it was a practical skill. When a loved one dies, respond by being more alive. Respond by finding more of yourself. Remember the elements you most enjoyed in your loved one. Talk to others who are grieving. Comfort them. It helps. Remember, life is all around you. Remember, loss is a long business (but not eternally sad). Remember, you can sing and laugh and grieve at the same time, because most things are more than one thing. All of us will leave this world, and the leaving is as striking and important as the arrival. Death, in all of its finality, is equally worthy of being celebrated. Death is a culmination of a powerful, intricate life force, death is a journey deep into the unknown, death is peace. Death is rest. Now your beloved is free from pain, fear, and the complexities of being awake in this realm. Passing on is a kind of freedom. Remember you are also free, as free as you will allow, and you are still here. Go on honoring their memory with newness and power. This feeling will change and so, indeed, will you.

Things as universal as death are great levelers. They bring humans closer in understanding with each other. Use them to connect with each other more deeply. We still do not have adequate language for most feelings, but we know them closely. We are, all of us, gold and silver mines of experience. We are conductors for all the things written in the body. This is how we touch each other. There is a reason why those who seem to have endured the most can be kindest, why those who have lost many things often find more and more of themselves. When you have suffered the absence of something you hold dear enough times, it deepens you. You learn the art of breathing through impermanent pain, and you begin to understand others who are feeling the same thing. Thick skin isn't always hard; mostly, it is made up of layer upon intricate layer of beauty, softness, and space.

Allow yourself space to process how you will—to access the full range that you are feeling. Grief is fluid, a thing of motion. It might be your first time experiencing this, and even if it is not, every single grief is new. Every day, note one word describing a feeling or sensation that is occurring inside you. The only rule is that it must be something different to what you wrote yesterday.

Allow yourself everything that will sweep over you. You will be surprised in this process by your capacity, surprised at the range of feelings available. Everything is a space for learning, even this. Every day, note one new thing that you know. The only rule is that it must be something different to what you realized yesterday.

Allow yourself the new things you reach for to express this grief. Every day, note one new thing that you feel moved to do, and do it. Don't judge yourself or your findings. Just keep noticing. The only rule is that it must be something different to what you did yesterday.

Bad News That Is (Sometimes) Good News

on moving on and perspective

There is no situation in all the world from which we do not garner something important, something to help ourselves or someone else. Most things are either something that you enjoy or something that will show you what you would prefer. No experience is useless. There is a way to use every last thing. Even when the happening itself is uncomfortable or difficult to understand, and wholly unwanted, there is always new information. This may seem like an outrageous concept and could even read as insensitive, but to consider things in this way is one of the most grounding and soothing gifts you may ever bestow upon yourself. Your world will not stop turning. Things will come, and come.

I had many experiences growing up and in early life from which I thought I would never recover. There they were, threatening to sink me because I could see no way to share them, largely out of fear and shame. But just because they felt awful does not mean they weren't useful. Every Last Thing I have experienced, whether joyful or otherwise, can be transmuted into something wonderful. We are all storytellers and story makers, whether we write or not. Our experiences help us to empathize and build understanding. They help us connect. Even the darkest and deepest of my secrets have helped me in writing, in truth telling, in deep loving. Often the most devastating circumstances to ever have befallen me have worked in a way to a kind of understanding, a connection to my fellow humans, a humility.

Consider your most challenging experiences and explore the opportunities that each one presents, for knowledge, for experience, for empathy, for sharing what you have learned with others. Look how many other paths they open up. Think about the gifts, in every scenario. This is a good space to involve your truthwork, to fold in the loving and transformative act of noticing, to consider showing up and understanding your purpose in new ways. Take time to consider this, as though your joy depends on it. It absolutely does.

SOMEBODY BETRAYED YOU—NO EXPERIENCE IS USELESS. YOU ARE JEALOUS—NO EXPERIENCE IS USELESS. YOU DIDN'T GET THE JOB—NO EXPERIENCE IS USELESS. THEY LOVE SOMEONE ELSE—NO EXPERIENCE IS USELESS. YOU DON'T LOVE THEM ANYMORE—NO EXPERIENCE IS USELESS. IT IS NOT AS YOU THOUGHT—NO EXPERIENCE IS USELESS. IT IS HARDER THAN YOU THOUGHT—NO EXPERIENCE IS USELESS. YOU MISS THEM—NO EXPERIENCE IS USELESS. YOU LOVE THEM—NO EXPERIENCE IS USELESS. THEY DON'T TREAT YOU WELL—NO EXPERIENCE IS USELESS. THEY WENT AWAY—NO EXPERIENCE IS USELESS. YOU ARE ALONE NOW—NO EXPERIENCE IS USELESS. BUSINESS CLOSURE—NO EXPERIENCE IS USELESS. NEW MANAGEMENT—NO EXPERIENCE IS USELESS. THE PLAN FAILED—NO EXPERIENCE IS USELESS. YOU HAVE TO START IT ALL AGAIN—NO EXPERIENCE IS USELESS.

When Nothing Works

everything is still working

On days resembling today, in times that look like now, you want to cry, or scream or shout, and nothing works. You're on the floor. You go to pray. The one who you are waiting for is busy on their knees. The forest is still living, still breathing in the distance, waiting for you to catch up to its complete and perfect knowing. You, on the ground, are a long way off. You breathe, or you try. Even breath is work. You want to eat, but nothing fills. You want to take several roads heading out of yourself. And nothing works. Some days it's all the wrong, wrong thing, and there will be no salve for it. There will be no book or song or verse for it—or there will be lots of words and a world of instruction but too much information, so nothing will work. Your lover will kiss you. Your child will tell you a funny story. Or there will be no lover and no child and no funny story. See, nothing works. But everything is still working. Feel everything. Resist nothing. Hold your stories and circumstances lightly, and without attachment. Treat them as waves in your glittering sea; both real and absurdly impermanent. The rain comes, in the end. For some it means joy. For others, disaster. Each one is as useful as the other, and neither is forever. You are not the same body of thoughts or things that walked you into this year. Most change happens slowly and in the excellent dark. Most large things are learned while we are busy with sleep. This is your life. You do not need to force it this way or that. There is a source running through you that is wiser than the head. Let go sometimes. Flow sometimes. Be a friend to your thoughts and let them rest. Are we not here, right now? Only we know How.

One Last Thing

Dear, Dear You.

This is a letter from your author, who, now I think of it, has been writing to herself by writing to you. Or is it the other way around? I am not sure. It is the early hours of February 11. It is my birthday. Outside, the sky is the singed, hopeful blue that appears just before the day erupts into cool, emerging light. Snow coats the pavement, and cloaks all unnecessary sound. Everything is white and quiet. It looks like I have reached the end for now, although honestly, I have barely scratched at it. I am now just understanding I could write for years and still not hit the breadth of what there is to be said. This is a strange feeling to have at the end of a book. Yet, as we know, the truth is written in and around our hearts, and anything I say can only ever serve as a reminder. Thoughts become something very different on the page, anyway, and almost everything ever written is poor translation. There is a reason the heart does not speak aloud. We would be immobilized by its beauty. Words make the work of our dreams touchable, somehow more concrete.

I did not write the book I imagined. I wrote mainly in fits and starts, in the dark hours of the morning. I could not see it becoming a book. I could not see it at all and yet something kept waking me up and guiding me to the pages, ahead of my inner critic. But the critic was there, alright. The critic woke up and came to find me. It hung around, unwelcome, and said things like, Why are you telling people what they already know? The critic knocked the ball out of my hands several times and never stopped. All I could do was play my music and carry on, and stop, and wonder what the point of anything was, and then carry on some more. I wrote from my own experience, as someone constantly wishing to follow my heart and always having to move myself out of the way. I wrote this as someone who does not have it worked out. I keep finding myself back at the beginning, which, oddly enough, is always new. Even as I write, I am still working my way out of many strange and distinct patterns, still unlearning several survival methods that try with all their might to hold me back. I grow weary running upon myself time and time again in the same dark corners of my mind, experiencing the very same setbacks and replaying old sequences. But each time I feel the old tightness, the worry, the existential unease, I know that something that I insist on doing is just not working. These days, I take any fatigue and depression to mean that I've traveled the same road one too many times. When I catch myself in some ideation or fantasy about giving up, or some desperate feeling of loneliness, I wonder what lie about myself I am making up. I wonder what I am forgetting.

There are, and there will be even more, days when we think we have figured it out. Days when we don't remember what was so hard about it all. Days when we are sure that it will be perfectly smooth sailing from here on in. And then, just like that, it falls apart again. Do I want to use the word *fail*? Fine. *Fail* is just another four-letter word that we vilify. I intend to fail as gorgeous foundation, fail as wind behind me, fail as the growing wild, fail as glowing ember, as starting point, as flickering lighthouse. Sometimes you think it's all over, when in fact you are standing at the edge of a new age. Old practices and patterns fall away because they must. They leave when it is time, and it is always Time.

Thank you for still being here.

Love, Always.
Yrsa Daley-Ward

Acknowledgments

With thanks to my editor, Meg Leder, for your love and belief in *The How* from the very first moment. For seeing these letters and understanding that they would become a book, long before I truly saw it. For asking the questions. Thank you for your attention and dedication, your encouragement, and, as ever, your kindness. Thank you to agent extraordinaire Marya Spence for your unique, exciting energy, always. I'm so grateful for you. Thank you to Lynn Buckley for the cover design, Patrick Nolan, and everyone at Penguin Books who made this come to life.

Thank you, thank you with all of my heart, to my beloved community online and offline. Your continued support and love mean much more to me than I could ever begin to express, and to those who have been here from the beginning, I treasure you completely. Jesh De Rox, you are a force. Leone Rose, to me you are amazing. Grandbrothers, you accompanied the construction of some of these sentences in ways that I cannot explain. Thank you also to my beautiful Constellation community. This book is dedicated to all of us.

And Dionne. This is for you. I know that I love you.

BONE

Foreword by Kiese Laymon

Bone. Visceral. Close to. Stark. The poems in Yrsa Daley-Ward's collection *bone* are exactly that: reflections on a particular life honed to their essence—so clear and pared down, they become universal. Each of the poems resonates to the core of what it means to be human.

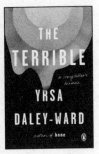

THE TERRIBLE

A Storyteller's Memoir

Through her signature sharp, searing poems, this is the story of Yrsa Daley-Ward and all the things that happened. "Even the terrible things. And God, there were terrible things." With raw intensity and shocking honesty, *The Terrible* tells the story of what it means to lose yourself and find your voice.